Climb Higher

Climb Higher

Reaching New Heights in Giving and Discipleship

Scott McKenzie
Kristine Perry Miller

ABINGDON PRESS

Nashville

CLIMB HIGHER

REACHING NEW HEIGHTS IN GIVING AND DISCIPLESHIP

This book is printed on acid-free paper.

Library of Congress Cataloging-in-Publication Data

McKenzie, Scott.
   Climb higher : reaching new heights in giving and discipleship / Scott McKenzie, Kristine Perry Miller.
      p.   cm.
   ISBN 978-1-4267-1483-2(book - pbk. / trade pbk. : alk. paper)   1. Christian stewardship. 2. Christian giving.   3. Christian life.   4. Mission of the church.   5. Christian leadership.   I. Miller, Kristine Perry.   II. Title.
   BV772.M3525 2011
   254'.8—dc22

                                                                          2011012882

11 12 13 14 15 16 17 18 19 20—10 9 8 7 6 5 4 3 2 1
MANUFACTURED IN THE UNITED STATES OF AMERICA

Contents

Introduction

At 29,035 feet, Mount Everest is the highest point on earth, and its summit is one of the destinations most sought after by adventurists. As described by a veteran climber, "No matter who you are, at what point in your life, weak, poor or afraid, Everest is our highest mountain and the climb has an everlasting, profound impact on most Everest [climbers' lives]."[1]

In this book, we use the acronym C.L.I.M.B., an abbreviation formed from the initial letters of our five chapters:

Clear and Compelling Vision

Leadership Development

Inspiration

Motivation

Boldly Ask

C.L.I.M.B. draws on an analogy comparing stewardship development and summiting Mount Everest. Both may seem to be long, challenging, and depleting endeavors, but for those who are successful, achieving the summit can be a life-transforming

Clear and Compelling Vision

Leadership Development

Inspiration

Motivation

Boldly Ask

experience. If you do an Internet search for "Mount Everest expeditions," you will discover several groups that will not promise to get you to the summit but will promise to give you the best *opportunity of* attaining the summit. For $60,000 to $65,000, you will be provided food, oxygen, tents, and most important, guides who have taken people to the top and back down. You will follow a team of Sherpas, native Himalayans who go before you, laying down thousands of feet of rope to guide you up to the summit as well as metal ladders to span the deadly crevasses that threaten climbers at every turn.

We believe the actions proposed by C.L.I.M.B. to be the equivalent of Himalayan Sherpas laying down the ropes and ladders to safely lead you to the summit, but this summit is that of effective stewardship. For those who are willing to do the work and commit to following C.L.I.M.B., achieving the summit of enduring and effective stewardship will have a profound and everlasting impact on you and the ministries of your church. Ministry will be funded and lives forever changed.

Just as the expedition guides dream of making Everest accessible to the masses, the components of C.L.I.M.B. are the result of a similar dream; a dream of a new reality. A reality in which

Christians no longer view "stewardship" as drudgery but as an exhilarating opportunity to develop a cherished relationship with Christ. A reality where people give joyfully, substantially, and gratefully to ministries that fulfill God's kingdom on earth. We dream of a

C.L.I.M.B. rejects all the negative baggage and instead presents stewardship as a life-giving, transformative process that results in deeper faith, stronger ministries, and vibrant congregations.

time when Christians live fully into the image of our generous and loving God.

If you are already living this reality, lay down this book and contact us immediately! If not, we hope this book will help move you and your congregation closer to this goal.

In each chapter we will focus on one element of the C.L.I.M.B. process, providing the theological foundation, wisdom gathered from our experiences working with hundreds of congregations, and some practical tools and templates for your use. Unlike most books written on the topic of stewardship, we provide comprehensive stewardship education as well as practical tools for your use. Remember, we are not only going to paint a glorious picture of the summit but also guide you there using the materials outlined in this book. While stewardship programs and fund-raising techniques will come and go, we believe the principles of

If you truly believe expressing generosity results in a deeper connection to God, you have no choice but to boldly ask others to become more generous givers.

C.L.I.M.B. to be foundationally true and lasting. As you build your stewardship ministry, your implementation of the processes will undoubtedly change, but the founding principles will remain the same.

Over the past years, and in fact decades, the term "stewardship" has garnered considerable negative baggage. Often the lowest position in the church leadership hierarchy, the stewardship chair is given the unenviable task of "raising enough money to fund the budget." We have worked with hundreds of stewardship chairs, and stories abound of their being avoided in church hallways and even losing long-term friendships—all in the name of stewardship.

Climb Higher was written with these folks in mind. C.L.I.M.B. rejects all the negative baggage and instead presents stewardship as a life-giving, transformative process that results in deeper faith, stronger ministries, and vibrant congregations.

C.L.I.M.B. contends that stewardship is *grounded in gratitude, revealed in prayer, and lived in faith.*

C.L.I.M.B. challenges the negative connotations associated with stewardship and invites congregations to completely change the conversation around this critically important topic. Instead of talking about the needs of the church budget, C.L.I.M.B. suggests a discovery of your congregation's compelling vision for ministry. Instead of selecting your stewardship leaders by default, C.L.I.M.B. encourages the development of strong leadership through setting clear and challenging expectations. C.L.I.M.B. involves changing the entire culture of your congregation to one of gratitude, where conversations revolve around sharing God's abundance rather than holding on fearfully. C.L.I.M.B. encourages the sharing of ministry stories rather than pledging to a budget. And, finally, C.L.I.M.B. asserts that if you truly believe expressing generosity results in a deeper connection to God, you have no choice but to boldly ask others to become more generous givers.

If you are ready to set out for the summit, keep this in mind: No teams successfully ascended the peak until the Sherpas had set fixed ropes and ladders.[2] We have worked with congregations and parishes all over the country, and we have set fixed ropes and ladders to assist you in your climb. We have described these "ropes and ladders" throughout each chapter of *Climb Higher*. Some concepts may be unfamiliar, and some may be downright scary. But we are convinced that if you trust the process and faithfully follow the ropes and ladders as outlined in this book, you will successfully achieve the summit of effective and lasting stewardship. As an Everest climber suggests, "Finally, Everest shows you the grace of great dreams, fears overcome and, sometimes, triumph following the most desperate of outlooks. This lesson is, perhaps, Everest's most powerful gift to all of us."[3]

CHAPTER ONE

Clear and Compelling Vision

I n the spring of 1996, more than thirty expeditions representing teams from America, Taiwan, Canada, New Zealand, South Africa, Japan, Russia, Tibet, Norway, and other locations camped on the flank of Everest at 17,600 feet. Though separated by nationality and language, their mission was the same—29,035 feet—to reach the summit. To accomplish this mission, one had to endure altitude sickness that could render a person unconscious; frostbite that made amputated toes and fingers a real possibility; and the fickle nature of Everest storms that could quickly turn a trip to the summit into a fight for one's life. Even after six climbers died in the spring of 1996, a seemingly endless stream of climbers, intent on reaching the pinnacle of Mount Everest, hiked past bodies still frozen in their final resting places. With such a visible reminder of the dangers of Everest in

In many churches, the "vision" seems to be nothing more than keeping the bills paid and the doors open.

front of them, why would they possibly continue? Two words—*the summit.*

In our combined twenty-five years of consulting with churches and a variety of nonprofit organizations, we have discovered compelling similarities between mountain climbing as described by Jon Krakauer in *Into Thin Air* and achieving the "summit" of effective and enduring Christian stewardship. While Christian financial stewardship education and annual commitment campaigns do not share the physical challenges and dangers of an assault on Everest, many pastors and the chairpersons of pledge programs can relate to these words by Krakauer: "I quickly came to understand that climbing Everest was primarily about enduring pain. And in subjecting ourselves to week after week of toil, tedium, and suffering."[1]

Whether conducting a Christian financial stewardship program or attempting to climb Mount Everest, having a clear and compelling vision is a crucial first step. In the not-so-distant past, clergy could announce to their congregations, "We need money for...," and, for the most part, people would contribute appropriately. But in the last few years the landscape has changed drastically, and the number of solicitations has grown exponentially. Between 2000 and 2009, the number of nonprofit organizations

(501[c][3]) in the United States increased from 819,000 to more than 1.2 million.[2] Now instead of one or two worthwhile organizations asking for charitable contributions, we are bombarded with requests from nonprofits

The most important question is, why? Why should I part with my hard-earned dollars? What will be the effect of my giving on people's lives?

every day. Organizations ask us to help find a cure for cancer or provide food and water to starving children. Pictures and videos of people who have suffered the effects of malnutrition or of birth defects create great emotion. A world where children have enough to eat and clean water to drink is a worthy goal. If a close friend or family member has been afflicted by an illness, prospective donors will likely have an affinity for supporting the organization that is trying to eradicate it. To everyone who has been touched by the effects of cancer, a cancer-free world is a compelling vision. A compelling vision inspires generosity.

And yet for many churches, when it comes time for the annual pledge program, the finance chairperson stands up and talks about how utilities have gone up, the pastor hasn't had a raise in three years, and how requests from the denominational headquarters have increased once again. In many churches, the "vision" seems to be nothing more than keeping the bills paid and the doors open. But is this really the vision God has for your church? Isn't God calling your church to be something more than a static place for maintaining your facilities and Sunday morning worship?

The most important question in any fund-raising program (church or otherwise) is not the question of how much—How much do I give? or How much do we need?—but instead the question is, why? Why should I part with my hard-earned dollars? What will be the effect of my giving to your organization? And much more important, what will be the effect of my giving on people's lives?

Perhaps one reason some congregations struggle to clearly articulate their vision is that they don't really believe that people's lives are being transformed as a result of their ministries. In one church where we worked, the congregation was trying to raise funds for a new building because they were out of space. One of the leaders said, "We can't advertise; we can't invite new people because we have no space, no place to put them." We asked them, "What if you knew you had the cure for cancer and decided to keep it to yourselves? Wouldn't that be unthinkable? Wouldn't that be almost criminal?" They nearly shouted back, "Of course!" So we asked another question: "Do you believe you have the answer for a world that is broken and hurting?" Again they answered, "Yes!" In the end, a clear and compelling vision for transforming lives led to a highly successful capital campaign for a new church building. Climbing the mountain of Christian financial stewardship requires a clear and compelling vision— and just paying the bills and keeping the doors open isn't it!

At this time, stop reading and reflect on the following questions:

1. How has your life or the lives of the people you love been transformed because of participation in the church?

2. What do you see happening in the lives of others that makes you excited about giving to your church?

Mission vs. Vision

In *A Spirituality of Fundraising*, Henri Nouwen says:

> Fundraising is proclaiming what we believe in such a way that we offer other people an opportunity to participate with us in our vision and mission. Fundraising is precisely the opposite of begging. When we seek to raise funds we are not saying, "Please could you help us because lately it's been hard." Rather, we are declaring, "We have a vision that is amazing and exciting. We are inviting you to invest yourself through the resources that God has given you—your energy, your prayers, and your money—in this work to which God has called us."[3]

Nurturing generosity in the church sends us back to the question of, What is this work that God has called us to? This is the question of mission and vision. Depending on the source, mission and vision can be described and defined in many different ways. For the purpose of C.L.I.M.B., our definitions are relatively simple. Mission is the basic and most fundamental reason we exist as a church. You might call it our unchanging driving force or our unyielding intent. The mission is the same for every Christian church in every denomination. Our mission is simple and was given to us in the Great Commission:

> Jesus came to them and said, "All authority in heaven and on earth has been given to me. Therefore go and make disciples of all nations, baptizing them in the name of the Father and of the Son and of the Holy Spirit, and teaching them to obey everything I have commanded you. And surely I am with you always, to the very end of the age." (Matthew 28:18-20 NIV)

As a church, the ultimate goal—the shared mission—is to make disciples. In our work, we have consulted with churches of different sizes, denominations, and traditions all over the country. From Protestants and Catholics in large megachurch settings to small urban and rural churches, all share the same mission—to make disciples. Different words may be used, but the mission is always the same—to create disciples for Christ.

Though we give voice to a shared mission, an unyielding intent, and a driving force of proclaiming the good news, when pushed most congregations admit to a very different reality. We often ask people in our churches to discuss the question, What is the actual driving force in your church? One way to encourage churches to be honest about this issue is to put the question to them this way: When a new program or ministry is brought to the governing board or council, what is the first question people ask? The response in hundreds of churches across the country has almost always been, How much is it going to cost? Never has a church responded that the number one question people ask when a new program or ministry is proposed is, How will this help us make disciples? or Is this what God wants? So while we may *think* our mission is to fulfill the Great Commission, the reality in many churches is that the driving force behind many stewardship programs is a plea for survival. Here is the budget. Here is what we need to survive. Would you please give to help us pay the bills?

Is it any wonder that many of our churches struggle to make ends meet?

While we may *think* our mission is to fulfill the Great Commission, the reality in many churches is that the driving force behind many stewardship programs is a plea for survival. Here is the budget. Here is what we need to survive. Would you please give to help us pay the bills?

At this time, stop reading and reflect on the following questions:

1. What is the driving force in your church? What is the unyielding intent for your church?

2. Name one time when people in your church stepped out in faith and did something they felt called by God to do. What happened?

The thirty-plus teams at the Everest base camp in the spring of 1996 shared a common mission—achieving the summit. Yet each team had a differing view of how they were going to reach their goal. Some of the guide groups provided the ropes, oxygen, tents,

> The mission is easy; after all, it's given in Scripture. The vision is the hard part. Discovering God's vision requires hard work, study, and prayer.

food, and supplies, but the climbers were on their own for the actual climb. Other groups made every effort to see that the climbers personally made it to the summit, even if that required putting a rope around them and pulling them up. The late Göran Kropp became a worldwide celebrity following his epic 1996 bicycle journey from his native Sweden to Nepal. He biked seven thousand miles, summited Everest without oxygen, then rode his bicycle home to Sweden again.[4] Göran Kropp shared the same mission, the same driving force as the other teams, but he had a very different vision of how he would reach the summit.

Effective stewardship programs require an unyielding desire to reach the summit, and also a compelling vision of how the mission will be accomplished. While creating disciples is the mission for every church, the vision, or implementation of this mission, is unique to each church. Many churches will spend months agonizing over the development of a mission statement and in the end come up with something that can be summarized as "Love God and love everyone else." Those who are really daring might say: "Worship God and serve others." After spending months coming up with their statement, they unveil it with pomp and circumstance, only to find the majority of the congregation very unimpressed and saying, "Tell us something we didn't know." The mission is easy; after all, it's given in Scripture. The vision is the hard part. Discovering God's vision requires hard work, study, and prayer.

Here are three simple questions to ask yourselves as a church body that will facilitate the development of vision:

1. Who are we?
2. What is our context or community for ministry?
3. What does God want?

Let's look at each of these questions individually.

Who Are We?

The first questions are, Who are we? What are our strengths and our weaknesses? What makes us truly unique in our community or area? To answer these questions you might want to begin by gathering some demographic material from your own members such as age, income, interests, and careers. Really get to know your people. Don't assume you know the actual makeup of your congregation. One congregation we worked with saw themselves as a retired, older congregation. After their research, they were shocked to discover a significant number of younger members in the church who were not in leadership positions. One easy way to get almost instant feedback on the question of, Who are we? is to do a quick survey using three-by-five-inch cards that are handed out at the end of the message or homily for two or three consecutive weeks.

The three-by-five-inch card may look something like this:

(Front of the card)

In an effort to understand the diverse needs of our congregation, we are gathering the following data. Please complete and return via the offering plate (one per member, please).

1. In which range does your age fall?

_____ 26 or younger

_____ 27 to 47

_____ 48 to 65

_____ 66 to 83

_____ 84+

2. How long have you been attending _____ Church?

_____ less than one year

_____ one to three years

_____ four to six years

_____ more than six years

3. In which ministries have you participated? (List your music groups, outreach, committees, etc.)

_____

_____

_____

_____

_____

(Back of the card)

4. What is your annual household income? [Include ranges that make sense for your congregation.]

_____

_____

_____

_____

_____

5. Other than its members, what do you consider the greatest strength of this congregation?

6. What do you consider this congregation's greatest opportunity for the future?

By allocating time during the worship service to complete the card survey, you will ensure the best possible response. Completing this exercise over two or three consecutive weeks covers those people who do not attend every Sunday. If you want to receive input from a broader base of your members, consider

To truly climb and successfully reach "the summit" requires a willingness to honestly evaluate not only who we are but also our strengths and our weaknesses.

conducting an online survey using Survey Monkey or another online survey company. Please see appendix A for Scriptures and message titles that would be appropriate for those two weeks.

Understanding who you are also involves examining your geographical location and physical plant. The vision of an older downtown church with no parking will be significantly different from that of a suburban church with ample parking and new, state-of-the-art facilities. Not better or worse, just different. Conduct a survey of your building and grounds while asking the question, How might both the strengths and weaknesses of our buildings influence or help define our specific vision? Here are some categories and questions you should consider:

Building Survey

Hospitality

1. When someone comes to worship for the first time, are they able to easily find your church? How could signage and lighting be improved to make your building stand out?

2. After a person arrives at your church, is he or she able to find the parking lot? Do you have spaces marked as reserved for visi-

tors? Are all the close spaces taken up so visitors are forced to park farther away?

3. Do your church grounds look well-tended and inviting? Does looking at your building from the outside make you want to see what's inside? Does it look like the people who attend your church care about its upkeep?

4. Is the main door easily identified? If you have several entrances, will people know which one to use?

5. Once inside, will a visitor be able to easily find her way to your nursery, classrooms, sanctuary, and restrooms? How can you improve your signage regardless of which entrance your visitors use?

6. Did you know that most visitors arrive just before (or in some cases, just after) the worship service begins? When they arrive in worship, is there a place near the back for them to sit?

7. What can you do to make your facility more available and accessible to visitors?

8. Is your parking lot or worship space at 80 percent of capacity? Statistics indicate that if that is the case, a visitor will determine the church is too full and will simply go home. Most will never return.

9. How welcoming is your nursery and children's church school space? Most parents of toddlers will choose whether or not to return to your church based on the condition of the nursery. It should feel homey, look up-to-date, and smell fresh.

Space Usage

1. How much of your facility is used? How much of the time? Are your classrooms, meeting rooms, and other spaces utilized to their capacity? Do you have room to spare?

2. Do you have land available adjacent to your property? Are there ways in which your land could be used for ministry (for example, outdoor meeting/worship space, children's activities, fellowship opportunities, fruit/vegetable garden for your community, and so on)?

3. Are there organizations in your community that have needs for the kinds of spaces you have available?

4. What programs or events could you host that would further your ministry objectives?

Strengths

What characteristics of your building are particularly noteworthy? How might they enable you to further your ministries?

Weaknesses

How could you improve the condition, size, or utilization of your facility to enhance ministries?

Vision requires us to take a look at ourselves, our facilities, and also our programming. What are your church's strengths and weaknesses in the area of programming? Are there significant gaps in terms of age-related ministries or programs? For example, some churches find they have a strong children's ministry but a weak or nonexistent ministry to seniors. And yet, as they look at their demographics, they often see a significant number of people over the age of seventy. Another way to address the question of programming and its potential effect on vision is by asking the questions, What do we do better than anyone else? What are we known for in our community or area? How might God be calling us to build on that strength? A note of caution: parishes that attempt to be all things to all people typically fail. Building on your strengths may require an objective review of all your ministries to determine which ones may no longer be a part of God's vision.

Let's return to the base camp at Everest. At base camp there were more than thirty teams with the same mission, the same purpose, the same unyielding intent—achieving the summit. However, before setting out for the summit, a clear and honest evaluation of each climber's strengths and weaknesses was required. If a climber had false perceptions of his strengths and weaknesses, not only would he be unlikely to attain the summit, but he might also jeopardize his life and the lives of his teammates. And in terms of Christian stewardship, to truly climb and successfully reach "the summit" requires a willingness to honestly evaluate not only who we are but also our strengths and our weaknesses.

What Is Our Context for Ministry?

The second question to ask is, What is our context for ministry? Any church that strives to achieve the summit of effective and enduring stewardship will continually be asking what God wants. In the language of climbing, you had better take the time

A compelling vision brings together the needs of the community or area with the strengths of the church. This intersection point of needs and strengths is the beginning of a vision that will inspire people!

to intimately know the terrain. The history of Everest abounds with stories of people with the mission, the unyielding intent, of reaching the summit. Most even had a vision of how to accomplish that mission. But only a few had enough knowledge of the mountain to make it happen. And therefore, many paid the ultimate price. Jon Krakauer tells the story of an Englishman named Maurice Wilson. It seems Wilson had the unyielding intent to climb Everest, and he even had a vision. He was going to buy an airplane, crash-land it into the side of Everest, and then climb to the summit. Unfortunately for Wilson, he soon learned that he could not receive permission to fly into Nepal. So he traveled to Tibet, where he was denied permission to enter. Finally he decided to hike more than three hundred miles to Everest disguised as a Buddhist monk. With no knowledge of mountain climbing and no knowledge of the perils of Everest, he began his assault on the great mountain. Amazingly, he made it to 22,700 feet. A later expedition team found his frozen body and buried it in one of Everest's icy crevasses.

Churches with an unyielding intent to disciple and be an instrument in the transformation of lives must be aware of the community in which they have been placed. They had better know the terrain and the weather patterns of their Everest. One little church outside Pittsburgh was absolutely convinced there were no young families or children in their community. They had convinced themselves that their community looked exactly like their members—old and gray. They began to look at "their mountain" and were shocked to discover that one of the largest demographic groups in their community was young families with children. A compelling and realistic vision demands an understanding of where God has placed us. At a minimum every church should be seriously looking at the census data for their particular area. Services such as Percept[5] provide more extensive data to help understand the demographics of your area, the primary concerns, and the anticipated growth patterns.

A key question is, How do the needs of the community intersect with your strengths? In other words, a compelling vision brings together the needs of the community or area with the strengths of the church. This intersection point of needs and strengths is the beginning of a vision that will inspire people!

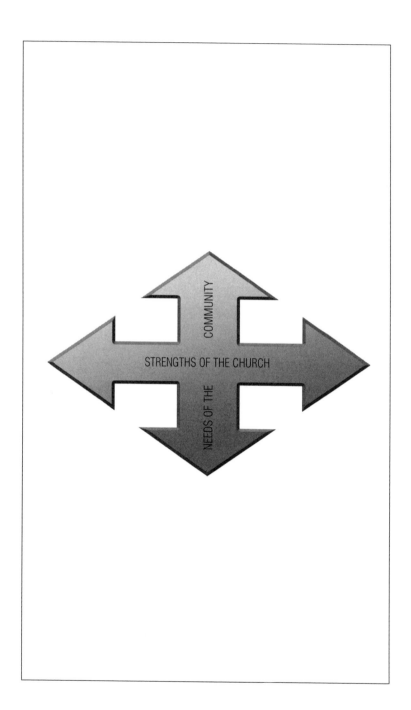

What Does God Want?

With a clear understanding of God's call to mission and ministry and with a unique vision that brings together the strengths of the church and the needs of the community, reaching the summit becomes a very real possibility.

The last question to be addressed might sound simple, but coming up with an answer may call for considerable time, study, and prayer. What does God want? In addressing this question we return to our discussion on mission and driving force. W. E. Deming, an American statistician, professor, author, lecturer, and consultant, was known to ask CEOs, "What business are you in?" If they were unable to answer the question, he said he couldn't help them. While some of our churches may have indeed forgotten their reason for existence, that does not mean effective stewardship is impossible.

We discover the answer to this question through a return to Bible study and prayer regarding the very reason we exist as a church. Consider conducting a Bible study focusing on the Great Commission and other Scriptures (see appendix A) that reflect the mission of your church. There are several books (see appendix B) that could also be used to inspire conversation and a clearer understanding of what God wants your church to do and why you exist. Remember this: without ownership of your vision and commitment to discerning God's will for the church, the rest of the process will not work.

The next step in answering the question, What does God want? is to prayerfully reexamine questions one and two: Who are we? and What is our context for ministry? Many churches discover their vision and specific call in the place where the responses to these questions intersect.

Our diagram now looks like this:

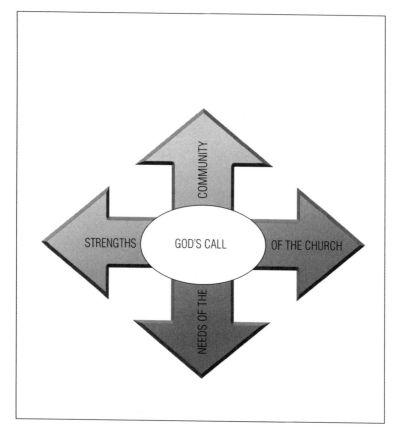

Let us illustrate how this played out in an actual church setting. When a Presbyterian church in Florida examined the demographics of their members, they discovered they were, essentially, a group of retired people, many with executive skills and abilities and most living away from their children and grandchildren. Most were spending the majority of their time in leisure activities. Then they began to look at their community demographics and discovered a large population of single mothers and people in the service industry. Many of these people were employed as gardeners, pool maintenance workers, and caregivers. At first the church members saw their age and demographics as being a barrier to mission and ministry. However, as the church members came to realize there is no retirement clause in the Great Commission, they realized their strengths matched the needs of their community, and a new vision for ministry was conceived. Their discussions turned to questions such as: What would happen if we adopted some of these young, struggling families and became their surrogate grandparents? What would happen if we became friends and mentors and shared our life experiences? The church day-care center, which they had previously considered an albatross and a money pit, was now seen as imperative and a central ministry for their future. Soon the path for achieving God's vision for their ministry became clear.

Make no mistake, attaining the summit of effective and enduring stewardship is no easy task. While not as physically challenging or as fraught with danger as attaining the summit of Everest, there are certainly unique issues and challenges that must be faced. With a clear understanding of God's call to mission and ministry and with a unique vision that brings together the strengths of the church and the needs of the community, reaching the summit becomes a very real possibility.

At this time, stop reading and reflect on the following questions:

1. What must happen in your church for you to seriously consider climbing the mountain of stewardship?

2. What are your unique challenges as you confront the issue of stewardship and a compelling vision for mission and ministry?

3. What are our unique strengths as we confront the issue of stewardship and a compelling vision for mission and ministry?

CHAPTER TWO

Leadership Development

ttaining the summit of effective and enduring stewardship requires a clear and compelling articulation of your congregation's vision for ministry. Simply knowing where God is leading you in your ministry will not, however, be enough to propel you to the top. Jon Krakauer writes:

Two hours into Thai flight 311 from Bangkok to Kathmandu, I left my seat and walked to the rear of the airplane...hoping to catch a glimpse of some mountains. I was not disappointed: there, raking the horizon, stood the jagged incisors of the Himalaya.... The ink-black wedge of the summit pyramid stood out in stark relief, towering over the surrounding ridges.... As I gazed across the sky at this contrail, it occurred to me that the top of Everest was precisely the same height as the pressurized jet bearing me through the heavens. That I proposed to climb to the cruising altitude of an Airbus 300 jetliner

A person in a leadership role who has not made a financial commitment to support the ministries of your church will derail your vision and be a stumbling block at every turn.

struck me, at that moment, as preposterous, or worse. My palms felt clammy.[1]

With God's vision for your congregation in front of you, contemplating the challenges of attaining enduring and effective stewardship may cause you to share Krakauer's sense of worry and concern. Even now your palms may feel clammy and your heart may be racing. Rest assured that, like Krakauer, you will be able to successfully achieve the summit, but doing so will require a committed and faithful leadership team.

So how can you be sure you are assembling the right leadership to serve on your stewardship committee? What attributes should you look for? What is the most effective way to recruit members to your stewardship ministry team?

If you were planning an expedition to the peak of Mount Everest, you would call on the most experienced and respected climbers to lead the way. Similarly, you will want to recruit your best stewards to lead you on the journey to the summit of enduring and effective stewardship. For some this may seem self-evident, but for others this has never been a consideration. In our experience, we have frequently seen stewardship committee members chosen without any consideration given as to whether or not they know anything about stewardship. In fact, in many cases, no one knows, including the clergy, if stewardship committee recruits are making a financial contribution to the operating budget. The most effective leaders will be those who are making significant investments in the fulfillment of your vision for ministry. This does not mean they will necessarily be making the largest contributions, but their gifts to your church should represent a meaningful and substantial commitment. A person in a leadership role who has not made a financial commitment to support the ministries of your church will derail your vision and be a stumbling block at every turn.

One church with whom we worked had recruited a bright young executive to serve as the chair of the stewardship committee. He was recruited because of his financial prowess and energetic nature, even though he had not made a financial commitment to the church's annual budget. The stewardship process he advocated consisted of a presentation showing the desperate nature of the church's budget followed by a plea for pledges to fund it. Not only did this approach have little to do with stewardship, but, as the chair, he was asking people to do something he was not already doing himself. Inexperienced stewards typically resort to a process focused more on a lack of funds than on a celebration of ministry. They tend to project all the reasons they are not contributing onto the rest of the congregation. In one instance, we heard a member of the stewardship committee blurt out in frustration, "Well, no one tithes; that's just ridiculous! Who would give away all that

Your stewardship committee needs to serve as ambassadors for the ministries of your church and share their enthusiasm with others as often as possible.

money?" When the process fails and the congregation responds poorly, the stewardship committee becomes deflated and frustrated. Often it takes years to get back on track, with opportunities to build ministry and grow spiritually lost forever.

As the spiritual leader of your congregation, clergy must also be practicing good stewardship by contributing substantially to the church's operating budget and being willing to share his or her stewardship story. If your clergy is not a role model for Christian financial stewardship, you will struggle mightily to succeed. Stewardship is a spiritual matter and must be addressed by your clergy, or you will be unlikely to ever leave "base camp."

Once you have identified those who are the good stewards, your next task is recruitment and setting expectations. What task are you recruiting them for? How will they go about accomplishing it?

Brilliant thinker and author Tom Peters has this to say about leadership:

> Sometimes I think that all "leadership literature" stinks—
> including much of the stuff I've written. Too much of the focus
> is on tactics and motivation (and frankly, manipulation). All
> of that misses the point: leadership for what? From King and

Gandhi and Jefferson . . . to Bill Gates and Steve Jobs and Richard Branson . . . leaders lead because they want to get some particular thing done. They want to do stuff that matters . . . great leaders are not merely great at "leading." They are great at inducing others to take novel journeys to places of surpassing importance.[2]

In recruiting members of your stewardship ministry team, you need to be clear about expectations. In the words of Tom Peters, "Leadership for what?" In many cases, prospective stewardship ministry team members presume they are being asked to raise enough money to fund the budget. The first objection typically raised is "I don't want to have to ask people for money." If raising money to fund the budget is the stated goal of your stewardship ministry team, you will have missed the point! Your stewardship ministry team is inviting people on a "journey to a place of surpassing importance"—to the summit of effective, enduring, and transformational Christian stewardship! Your stewardship ministry team is being asked to inspire others to do "stuff that matters."

Invite your prospective team members to join you with the following goals in mind:

1. Assist in leading the congregation in fulfilling God's vision for the congregation's ministries.

2. Help people discern God's will for their resources.

3. Encourage people to become closer to God by imitating God's generous nature.

When we are generous, we are most like God.

The first task of your stewardship team is to assist in leading the congregation in the fulfillment of its God-given vision for ministry. In the previous chapter, we discussed the need for each congregation to discover its own clear and compelling vision for ministry. Ideally your stewardship committee members have been involved in the process of discovering this vision. Regardless, your stewardship committee needs to serve as ambassadors for the ministries of your church and share their enthusiasm with others as often as possible. God has given you a vision for ministry—God has called your congregation to do something miraculous! Whether it is to serve the homeless, to evangelize with a rockin' contemporary service, or to create the most awesome youth program, God has called you to do something special. Your stewardship team should be prepared to show up, to advocate for the vision, and to passionately support your church's ministries.

The second role of the stewardship ministry team is to encourage others to seek God's will for the resources they have been given. In other words, to seek divine inspiration. This is a significant change in perspective from where we started—a stewardship committee whose goal it was to fund a budget. For the journey toward generosity to be successful, we need to experience and express gratitude for all God has given. While all elements of stewardship development are important, the element most often overlooked is prayer. Our experience tells us that Christians believe prayer works. When people take seriously the call to prayer, God often moves them in a direction they had never considered. In other words, God often moves us to greater levels of commitment and generosity. When people take prayer seriously, they quickly come to realize that God has given them self, life, breath,

If we tell prospective committee members that the role really isn't as big as they imagine, the time commitment is less than they think, and they can probably miss about half the meetings and still serve, what does this say about the importance of the role they are being asked to fulfill?

energy, wealth, and time to be used for God's purposes rather than their own. Seeking inspiration is the role of your stewardship team. We will talk more about inspiration in chapter 3.

Finally, the role of the stewardship committee is to take others on a journey resulting in a closer connection with God. Instead of viewing stewardship as a way to convince people to give more money, view the role of the stewardship committee as a way to inspire people to become more generous. As you are learning more about this concept of stewardship, remember that God does not want or need our stuff, he simply wants us to need it less. If we are created in the image of a generous and loving God, then we are inherently generous and loving. Doesn't it follow then that when we are generous, we are most like God? The role of the stewardship committee is to help people express their godlike nature—to be loving and generous.

So how should you go about recruiting stewardship committee members and conveying the tasks they are being asked to accomplish? In our experience, stewardship committee members are often selected not because of their particular skill sets, but because they are most likely to say yes. The "usual suspects" or sometimes people new to the church are selected—assuming their eagerness to be of service will overcome their ignorance about stewardship formation issues. Sometimes, in an effort to encourage someone to accept a leadership role, we even downplay the commitment in hopes of filling a position, regardless of the person's fit for the role. We tell prospective committee members that the role really isn't as big as they imagine, the time commitment is less than they think, and they can probably miss about half the meetings and still serve. What does recruiting like this say about the importance of the role they are being asked to fulfill? How important could the task be if it can be accomplished with only a halfhearted effort? Can you imagine recruiting a team to climb Everest in the same halfhearted way? When recruiting your stewardship team, be clear about the tasks they are being asked to fulfill. This is not about funding the church budget. This is about discovering God's vision for your ministry and inviting your congregation to prayerfully consider how they are called to invest in its fulfillment. You are asking your stewardship ministry team to be leaders on a journey to the summit of effective, enduring, and transformational stewardship! This journey will require their faithful dedication and some hard work, but reaching the summit is well worth the effort. This is truly "stuff that matters."

At this time, stop reading and reflect on the following questions:

Equipping your leaders with an understanding of Christian stewardship will not only set a better foundation for their ministry but also build more-committed disciples for your congregation.

1. How have you typically recruited stewardship committee members? What attributes did you identify as important?

2. How can you better identify committed and faithful leadership for your stewardship committee?

3. How will you communicate the tasks of the stewardship committee?

Practical Ideas for Attaining the Summit with Effective Leadership

Once you have your stewardship leaders on board, you will want to train them well for the tasks they are asked to accomplish. Do not make assumptions about what your leaders know or do not know about the theology of stewardship. It is likely that those within your group will possess various levels of knowledge and understanding about stewardship, especially if they have come from different denominational backgrounds. While some may have insightful opinions, others may have ideas borne out of previous experiences where stewardship efforts have been manipulative or even offensive. Equipping your leaders with an understanding of Christian stewardship will not only set a better foundation for their ministry but also build more-committed disciples for your congregation.

A book or DVD study is a great way to share some ideas about Christian stewardship and invite discussion. Several resources are suggested (see appendix C), but there may be others you wish to consider. Once you decide on a book or DVD, plan to take a few minutes at the beginning of each meeting to review. During your discussions, you will want to make sure everyone has the opportunity to have his or her opinion heard. Some who are silent may still be carrying around baggage and perhaps anger about past stewardship efforts gone awry. Drawing these experiences out and allowing people to share will enable your group to view stewardship in a much more positive light. Your conversations may take several months, and if so it will be time well spent. If you're typically conducting a fall pledge program, try to have your book or DVD study complete by August, as this will allow you time to plan your pledge program accordingly. If you are fortunate enough to have planned ahead and are selecting your materials in January, you will have plenty of time to complete your study before designing your stewardship process.

Some churches with whom we have worked invited the congregation to participate in the book or DVD study with very positive results. Adult education sessions devoted to lively discussions about stewardship-related topics will increase understanding and educate your congregation. Whether you choose a book or DVD series, the important thing is to engage your congregation in conversation to deepen their understanding of what it means to be good stewards of God's gifts.

Another way to inspire conversation about stewardship is to develop a "Leadership Stewardship Statement." Not to be confused with a mission statement or a vision statement, the Leadership Stewardship Statement is a one-page articulation of your stewardship committee's view of stewardship. In developing this document, your discussion will enable you to hear and respond to various points of view, as well as encourage thoughtful consideration of what being a good steward actually means. You will need to set aside about an hour and provide some examples from which to work (see appendix D). Ask your board or stewardship committee to pick out words or phrases from the examples given. Now invite them to change some of the phrases that don't resonate as well with them and build your Stewardship Statement from there. After you have spent an hour or so, have someone compile your notes and write a first draft. Edits or comments can be solicited via e-mail, so your next meeting can be spent fine-tuning. Once you have a final version of your Stewardship Statement, it will be time to share it with your entire congregation. Enlarge your Stewardship Statement and post it on a piece of foam-core board along with the signatures of those who created the statement. Introduce the Stewardship Statement to your congregation during worship and explain the development process you went through. Place the mounted Stewardship Statement in a high-traffic area in the church and invite others to read and sign it too. You may also want to post your Stewardship Statement on your website and include it in your newsletter or bulletin. Your Stewardship Statement will be a powerful declaration from your church's leadership to the congregation.

Stewardship testimonies or witnesses are another powerful way in which to enlighten your congregation. Those who have been practicing good stewardship for a long time have been on a spiritual journey and have learned many lessons along the way. Your pastor should offer a personal testimony first as a witness to his or her beliefs and practices. Next, invite your experienced stewards to share their stories with the congregation. Testimonies may be given by singles, couples, and members of your youth group. Invite them to consider some or all of the following as they prepare their remarks: Who taught you about giving? How has giving helped you grow spiritually? What lessons have you learned on your journey? Speakers should be asked to model for others the elements of Christian stewardship—gratitude, prayer, and faith. Testimonies can take place in worship, small-group meetings, or through written newsletter articles. Encourage your speakers to limit their testimony to three minutes and write them down in advance. This will keep your speaker on track and keep worship running on time, even when emotions run high. It has been our experience that those who share their testimonies are as blessed in telling them as those are who hear them.

With a committed group of people who understand steward-ship and are committed to the objectives of the stewardship process, you will be well on your way to the summit of enduring and effective stewardship.

CHAPTER THREE

Inspiration

Yes, nurturing generosity calls for a clear and compelling vision. And yes, growing in faith requires committed and capable leadership. But more than anything else, to attain the summit of enduring and effective stewardship requires inspiration. There comes a time in every climb when the winds blow, the peak is obscured by clouds, the legs ache, and the lungs are on fire. At this moment it is not about tactics or method; it is about finding "something more." That "something more" is inspiration!

The meaning of *inspiration*, according to the Online Etymological Dictionary, is "the immediate influence of

We are inspired to give, meant to give, and in the giving we are inspired or animated with new life. In our giving we become like God.

God or a god...to inflame, to blow into, to breathe...to influence with or animate with an idea or purpose." If vision is the catalyst for stewardship, then inspiration is the life-giving force. Inspiration is crucial to stewardship because we know God is the giver of all things, and when we seek God's guidance for the use of these gifts, we find ourselves in closer relationship to God. Ultimately, we are most alive when we embody the God-given characteristics of generosity.

The most frequently quoted verse of Scripture is John 3:16: "For God so loved the world that he..." What did God do because of his love? God *gave*. Notice the sequence. First God loved; then, out of this great love, God gave. And what he gave was incredibly precious—himself.

In a stewardship program infused with inspiration and grounded in allowing the breath of God to blow into people's hearts, we move from searching for the right program, the right letter, or the right sermon to an entirely new way of thinking about who we are and what we are called to do. Winston Churchill reputedly said, "We make a living by what we get. We make a life by what we give." Giving is life-giving. We are inspired to give, meant to give, and in the giving we are inspired or animated with new life. In our giving we become like God.

At this time, stop reading and reflect on the following questions:

1. Think of a time when you were truly inspired to give— to be deeply and extravagantly generous.

2. What was it like? Can you recall the joy, the sense of being alive with purpose and meaning when you gave?

3. What led you to that point? How were you changed?

When people become inspired—led by the Holy Spirit—something truly transformational occurs. In our work we have witnessed numerous conversions because people took seriously the invitation to prayer and allowed the life-giving breath of God to guide their giving. Take Jim, for example. Jim was a successful entrepreneur and a peripheral member of a Catholic church in the Midwest. In the early stages of his parish's capital campaign, Jim was contemplating a contribution of $10,000 over a three-year period—certainly substantial, but to Jim, not much of a stretch. Jim took part in the campaign by volunteering his time to mail campaign materials to members and, eventually, became one of the campaign's key spokespersons. As the campaign progressed, Jim took seriously the invitation to invite God into his decision about how much to contribute to his parish. When he did, something, or rather Someone, inspired Jim to contribute more than he'd ever imagined possible. In the end, Jim gave generously and contributed $50,000 to his parish. This experience was so transformational that in a future capital campaign, Jim served as the director and made a gift of $100,000 to the effort. Jim would be the first to tell you God had gotten hold of his heart and inspired his giving. Jim's journey of faith changed his life forever.

Jim experienced what Henri Nouwen describes as conversion.

Fundraising is also always a call to conversion. And this call comes to both those who seek funds and those who have funds. Whether we are asking for money or giving money we are drawn together by God, who is about to do a new thing through our collaboration.... To be converted means to experience a shift in how we see and think and act.... It is a shift of attention in which we set our mind on divine things.... Fundraising as ministry involves a real conversion.[1]

Without inspiration, without a focus on life-changing conversion, stewardship programs can become manipulative and in the worst cases coercive. When we were working with a large congregation in Colorado, an older woman approached with tears in her eyes and shared her story. During a previous capital campaign, she said, church members had been told how much they should contribute and were expected to comply. Being coerced in this way made her feel angry and hurt. As a result, she chose to contribute nothing to her church. In hearing how the current campaign would be focused on inspiration, she was relieved and grateful. By participating in a campaign that was based on inspiration rather than coercion, she chose to contribute generously. Her gift became an expression of her gratitude to God, had been revealed to her in prayer, and was offered as an act of faith. She went on a journey to the summit of enduring and effective stewardship. In order for stewardship programs to have an enduring and effective outcome—to attain the summit—they need to be inspired by God. Stewardship is about conversion, about God blowing the breath of life into people's hearts and wallets.

Consider this definition of Christian stewardship: *grounded in gratitude, revealed in prayer, and lived in faith.* Inspiration is foundational—and gratitude is the key to inspiration. If you want to make stewardship formation effective and enduring, if you want to attain the summit, create a culture of gratitude.

If you are serious about attaining the summit of enduring and effective stewardship, you need to create a culture of gratitude.

Gratitude

Gratitude, according to Henri Nouwen, flows from the recognition that who we are and what we have are gifts to be received and shared.[2] True inspiration to give and be generous occurs when we realize that all we have and all we are is a gift from God. When we acknowledge God's abundant gifts, we become grateful. Gratitude incites generosity. In fact, a truly grateful heart will have no alternative but to be a giving and generous heart. Take Millie, for example. Millie had very little in practical, financial, worldly terms. But Millie had a heart that was absolutely overflowing with gratitude. When Millie got up every morning she was indeed grateful for being alive. If the sun was shining, Millie was grateful for the warming sunlight. If it was raining, Millie was grateful for the life-giving rain. Millie could sing the praises of a bright yellow dandelion in the middle of a green yard or the beauty of a rose cultivated in a nursery. In the midst of one of her church's stewardship programs, Millie was determined to make a generous financial gift in spite of her limited means. Church members and pastors tried to talk Millie out of making the gift, telling her, "You've done enough, Millie; you need the money for yourself." Millie was indignant. "How dare you deny me the joy of giving when God does so much for me every day?" For Millie, her grateful heart had no choice but to respond generously.

This intimate connection between gratitude and generosity became even clearer during a mission trip. As a middle-class, well-fed American preaching and helping distribute food in the African country of Malawi, I had the opportunity to see a culture of gratitude firsthand. In 2003, Malawi ranked 162 out of 179 countries in the United Nations human development survey. In the rural villages nearly every family had been affected by either famine or AIDS or, many times, both. I held children with distended bellies on my lap and saw the quiet despair of their mothers who were unable to feed them and forced to watch them slowly starve. And yet, inevitably as we prepared to leave every village, the people would come forward singing, clapping, and bringing us gifts from their meager gardens. We were surprised, perplexed, and perhaps a bit angry until our host, a local pastor, said to us, "You must accept their gifts. You see, they are so very grateful that you cared enough to come, they need to give you something, and this is all they have."

Think for a moment about those words spoken by that pastor in Malawi: *They are so very grateful . . . they need to give you something.* Gratitude compels us, drives us to higher levels of generosity.

At this time, stop reading and reflect on the following questions:

Why not kick off your stewardship process by inviting the congregation to fill out gratitude cards that ask people to identify ways in which they have been blessed, the things they are most grateful for?

1. Recall a time when you were nearly overcome with a profound sense of gratitude. What were the circumstances?

2. Were you inspired in any way to do something, say something, or change something?

Creating a Culture of Gratitude

In 1996, the United States Conference of Catholic Bishops published a pastoral letter on stewardship called *Stewardship: A Disciple's Response.* They say this about gratitude: "Good stewards live with joy and gratitude for the blessings they have received—including those that have multiplied through diligence and hard work."[3]

If you are serious about attaining the summit of enduring and effective stewardship and unwilling to settle for the base camp of short-term, quasi-effective fund-raising, you need to create a culture of gratitude. In the words of the Catholic bishops, we need to help people "live with joy and gratitude for the blessings they have received." The first task in creating such a culture is to help people identify the many ways in which they are truly blessed. Why not kick off your stewardship process by inviting the congregation to fill out gratitude cards? Typically, you ask for commitment/pledge cards, but how about beginning your program with a card that asks people to identify ways in which they have been blessed, the things they are most grateful for? Precede the completion of gratitude cards with gratitude testimonies from people like Millie or people who have been to places like Malawi. This is a great place to involve children and teens by inviting them to complete gratitude cards and provide gratitude testimonies. One church had people complete their gratitude cards in worship and process them forward to be blessed on the altar. The gratitude cards were then posted on portable walls in the narthex/gathering space, where people could spend time reading them before and after worship. Another Catholic parish published in their newsletter the responses of their school's elementary-age children. A third-grade child wrote that she was thankful for her school because she loved recess, lunch, and had met Jesus there. Talk about inspiration!

One of the best ways to create a culture of gratitude is to practice and demonstrate gratitude. One church created a Gratitude Committee because they felt it was important to find as many ways as possible to say thank you. During an annual stewardship program, most churches will assemble a team to make calls to people who have not yet made a pledge. Why not ask your leadership board or Gratitude Committee to make phone calls to people who support the parish with gifts of time or money? Would your people appreciate receiving this type of call? "No, I am not calling to ask you for anything. I am just calling to say thank you for the week you gave for vacation Bible school." Create a culture of gratitude, and you will go a long way toward attaining the summit of enduring and effective stewardship.

Prayer

Remember our phrase: *grounded in gratitude, revealed in prayer, and lived in faith.* Creating a culture of gratitude will move and inspire people to be generous with their time, talents, and treasures. From gratitude we move to prayer as we ask, "God, based on all you have done for me, all that I have to be thankful for, what would you now have me do?" Through prayer God helps us discern what to do with all of our blessings and resources. Through prayer God reveals how our resources can best be used to build the Kingdom: "Ask, and it will be given you; search, and you will find; knock, and the door will be opened for you. For everyone who asks receives, and everyone who searches finds, and for everyone who knocks, the door will be opened" (Matthew 7:7-8).

We believe one word underlies a true life of prayer. This one word is in fact the secret to spiritual growth and maturity. From

Abraham to Moses and eventually Jesus himself, a one-word description of their relationship to God is "willing." Abraham was called by God to go, and he went. Moses was called to lead and, after offering all his excuses, he led. In the garden Jesus said, "Father, I don't want to do this, but none the less, not my will but yours be done" (see Luke 22:42). He was willing to take the cross. True and effective prayer is ultimately about an openness and willingness to listen and then respond to the call of God.

Most of us spend our lives in one of two places: being either will-less or willing. To be will-less is to say, "I can't do that, and you can't expect me to do that." In stewardship terms it is exemplified by the notions:

- I can't give because I am on a fixed income.
- I can't give because I have small children and we are saving for college.
- I can't give because my children are in college.

Pretty soon all of life is an "I can't do it," and there is no good time for giving. In one church, a key leader in the campaign named Linda was struggling with her ability to make a gift to the church's capital fund drive. In one conversation, she expressed her desire to give but went on to list the multiple reasons she would be unable to do so. All of them were quite legitimate: her pay had been cut recently, a child was headed to college in the fall, and another child needed new braces. Linda was mired in a state of will-lessness. We reminded her that all she was being asked to do was to be open to God's leading and be willing to pray. This eased her concerns somewhat, and Linda vowed to pray for God's guidance in her giving. Several weeks later, Linda was like a new person with renewed energy and spirit. Shortly after her commitment to prayer, Linda received a letter from an attorney telling her she would receive a small inheritance from her grandfather. The last time she had been

> **From the very beginning of a stewardship program, when you create a sacred space and opportunity for people to pray, a place for people to both listen to and respond to the call of God, miraculous things can occur.**

with her grandfather, he had been on his last construction job. He was building a church. Linda remarked, "I can't believe that while my granddaddy was building that church, God was providing a way for me to help build mine." Through prayer, Linda went from being will-less to willing. Inspiration enabled Linda to make a generous gift to her church and reach the summit of enduring and effective stewardship.

While some people are will-less, there are also those who are will-full. Will-full is an attitude that says, "I know exactly what I can afford to comfortably give. I have decided on the amount of my pledge, and no one, not even God himself, will move me off that number. There is no need to pray, no need to be open. This is all I am able to do." In contemplating his gift to support the building of his church's new parish hall, Jeff had carefully

Create a culture of gratitude, prayer, and willingness, and you will find yourself well on the way to the summit of enduring and effective stewardship.

examined his family's budget, done a spreadsheet with income and expenses, and decided they could come up with an extra $10,000 over the next three years. Period! No more. But then Jeff began to go on the journey, and he began to pray. Jeff would be the first to tell you that he is not a praying man, but he and God would "chat a bit" as he took his morning shower. Eventually, Jeff's wife, Nancy, threatened to cut off his hot water because Jeff's "chats with God" had caused his pledge amount to increase by five times. With a laugh she said, "I can't afford any more hot showers." Both Jeff and Nancy became inspired—their lives became alive and animated with the breath of God. They had made the journey from will-full to willing through openness and prayer.

This emphasis on prayer and being willing is not just about dollars and cents. It is also about the use of time and talent—life itself. During the midst of stewardship programs, we have seen individuals called by God into ordained ministry, marriages reconciled, people starting new careers and opening new businesses. Why? Because from the very beginning of a stewardship program, when you create a sacred space and opportunity for people to pray, a place for people to both listen to and respond to the call of God, miraculous things can occur. From gratitude, through prayer and willingness, people and churches are led on a wonderful journey that leads to the summit of enduring, effective, and life-changing stewardship.

A word of caution: Your stewardship committee and leadership board have the responsibility to honor any gift, pledge, or decision determined through prayer. If someone decides not to contribute to a financial stewardship effort or declines a leadership position, that decision must be honored. A prayerful, heartfelt answer of no is better than a decision made as a result of guilt, pressure, or manipulation.

At this time, stop reading and reflect on the following questions:

1. Try to recall one time when you were intentional about listening for God's will for your life. What happened?

2. Reflect on a time when you moved from being either will-less or will-full to willing. What happened?

Creating a Culture of Prayer and Willingness

Creating a culture of prayer begins with a personal commitment from your leadership to pray. From the beginning of your stewardship process, clergy, church leaders, and stewardship committee members should commit to praying for God's guidance in the use of their time, talents, treasure, and involvement. Your leadership should also be willing to speak about their commitment to prayer and their willingness to be open to God's leading. Your leaders should be willing to lead people on the journey by setting the tone for prayer throughout your stewardship process. Do not allow secular influences to take you off course. A commitment to prayer is one of the most important elements of your stewardship efforts—the key to success on your journey to the summit of effective and enduring stewardship. The Conference of Catholic Bishops' statement on stewardship says the following:

> A bishop's or pastor's prayerful meditations on Christian stewardship should precede the start of a diocesan or parish stewardship program. Prayer becomes a potent and precious resource for the process because the primary objective in stewardship education is always a renewal of commitment to Christian discipleship. To be successful, stewardship education requires the bishop or pastor to make a complete, constant, personal, and official commitment to stewardship as a constitutive element of Christian discipleship. A bishop or pastor who does not have a solid conviction about the importance of stewardship will give only halfhearted support to the stewardship programs of his diocese or parish. The results will reflect this lack of total commitment.[4]

In this section, the bishops are referring to the centrality of prayer for pastors and bishops in the stewardship process, but this concept also applies to the entire congregation. Do you really want someone in any leadership position if they are unwilling to commit to prayer? Along with creating the expectations for prayer, clergy and lay leadership should also be willing to provide teaching and training in prayer. Any leadership meeting, any gathering for administration, becomes an opportunity to teach about prayer and willingness. In some churches, the committee chair or pastor lights a candle for any administrative gathering as a reminder that God is front and center. Instead of a strict compliance to *Robert's Rules of Order*, some churches are moving toward the idea of discernment and consensus in the decision-making process. Some church committees have included "prayerful pauses" every thirty min-

One of the key questions to consider is this fundamental question of faith: Does the gift you are contemplating represent faith? If giving this gift is fairly easy and comfortable, perhaps it does not represent a gift of faith and trust. If the gift is one that causes you to change your lifestyle or to trust in God to help fulfill it, then it is a gift given in faith and trust.

utes or so to invite God into their meetings and to listen for God's leading. Creating a culture of prayer and willingness begins with your leadership.

Just as we used gratitude cards and gratitude testimonies, the same can be used effectively for prayer. Before any significant event in the church's life, not just your stewardship program, distribute prayer commitment cards and ask everyone to pray each day leading up to the event. At the conclusion of the event, invite people to give testimonies about the difference prayer made. Prayer vigils can be an excellent way to engage people in prayer for any event and will enable you to involve people of all ages, including your children and youth. Several churches have used prayer stones during the course of their capital campaigns. Each person is given a river stone on which they write their name as a statement of their commitment to pray for the church. The stones are cast into the footers and foundation of the new building. The building is then literally built on the prayers of the people. Create a culture of gratitude, prayer, and willingness, and you will find yourself well on the way to the summit of enduring and effective stewardship.

A culture of gratitude and prayer will create inspiration, but it is the next part of the phrase that may propel you to the summit: *grounded in gratitude, revealed in prayer, lived in faith.* Ultimately, enduring and effective stewardship is about how we live. Gratitude and prayer are simply pious platitudes if they do not change or impact the way we live our lives. Effective stewardship always presents the opportunity and challenge for people to step out in faith and do something they would have never thought possible.

One of the key questions to consider is this fundamental question of faith: Does the gift you are contemplating represent faith? If giving this gift is fairly easy and comfortable, perhaps it does not represent a gift of faith and trust. If the gift is one that causes you to change your lifestyle or to trust in God to help fulfill it, then it is a gift given in faith and trust. Consider the definition of *faith* found in Hebrews 11:1: "the assurance of things hoped for, the conviction of things not seen." The most precious gift is the gift that comes as a result of such faith. Time and time again we hear people say, "This is the gift we are going to make. We are not sure how it will happen, but we make it in faith.

> **Creating a culture of faith is about helping people step out of their comfort zones and into whatever they feel touched or called by God to do.**

Because of our gratitude for all that God has done and after prayer and openness, this is what we are called to do."

Rev. Blessings Magomero is a pastor, host, and guide to many groups who do missionary work in Malawi. Recently, he moved to the United States to attend school. After spending some time in the States he observed, "I know why Americans have such little faith and trust. They don't have to have faith. They already have everything they need." Perhaps that is the real reason stewardship is such a powerful opportunity for personal change and transformation. For some people it is the first time they are asked, in a concrete way, to step out of their comfort zone and do something that truly requires faith and trust.

Faith

The creation of a culture of faith occurs as a congregation develops a culture of gratitude and prayer. We are grateful for all God has

The church or parish that deliberately works at creating a culture of gratitude, prayer, and faith will offer to its members one of the greatest gifts imaginable: the knowledge that their truest and deepest identities reside in being like God

given. We have prayed for a spirit of openness and willingness. Now what? The "now what?" may be participating in a mission trip. The "now what?" may be filling out a pledge card for the first time or making a commitment to begin tithing. The "now what?" may be participating in an in-depth Bible study. The "now what?" may be agreeing to serve on a committee for the first time. The "now what?" may be going to an estranged relative or friend and asking for forgiveness or offering forgiveness. Creating a culture of faith is about helping people step out of their comfort zones and into whatever they feel touched or called by God to do.

In a church where we worked we met Steve, who stepped out of his comfort zone when he felt touched by God. As a construction worker, truck driver, and race-car aficionado, Steve had little time for church. But because of his daughter's involvement, Steve became involved in church, and on one particular Sunday, he found himself in the strange position of being divinely nudged. A mission trip had been announced and volunteers were being enlisted. After a few long weeks, Steve timidly approached the pastor and described not so much a divine nudging as a divine bludgeoning. Steve, who had never been outside his home state, soon found himself an ocean away, in a country unknown to most people. During the mission trip, Steve's faith blossomed and his tough exterior grew soft. His willing spirit resulted in a closer connection to God and a journey of faith.

One of our favorite stories is of the golden Buddha of Bangkok. When the Burmese were about to attack the city, the solid-gold Buddha was covered in mud plaster to hide its value. Two centuries later, still encased in mud, the Buddha was thought to be worth very little. But in 1957, when the Buddha was being moved to a new temple in Bangkok, it slipped from a crane and was left in the mud by workmen. In the morning a temple monk, who had dreamed the statue was divinely inspired, went to see the Buddha. Through a crack in the plaster he saw a glint of yellow and discovered that the statue was pure gold. It's now officially the world's largest solid-gold Buddha at nearly ten feet high and weighing more than five tons.

We have discussed how inspiration is that which brings the breath of life and how stewardship is intimately related to conversion. Remember John 3:16? We were created by God as sacred and holy, created to be like him, generous and giving. But during the course of our lives something happens and we find ourselves encased by the mud of selfishness, materialism, and the insatiable desire to acquire more. However, stewardship, and in particular inspiration, chips away at the mud and allows the beauty of generosity to be revealed in all its glory. The church or parish that deliberately works at creating a culture of gratitude, prayer, and faith will offer to its members one of the greatest gifts imaginable, the knowledge that their truest and deepest identities reside in being like God—loving and generous. When that gift is offered and received, the summit will be well within reach.

CHAPTER FOUR

Motivation

For those of us who have never considered tackling anything as challenging as an assault on Mount Everest, it is difficult to imagine what would motivate someone to go through such a grueling and dangerous experience. In *Into Thin Air*, Jon Krakauer writes, "It struck me that most of us were probably seeking, above all else, something like a state of grace."[1] While backgrounds, experiences, and personalities varied dramatically, each climber was motivated to achieve the summit, hoping to experience something truly transformational. The long and often arduous journey would be worth the effort to experience this life-changing accomplishment.

For most of your church members, a plea to increase giving in order to cover increasing costs does little to inspire generosity.

Just like Krakauer and his fellow climbers, you are embarking on a journey that may be challenging and perhaps even frustrating. But know that when you reach the summit of effective and enduring stewardship, the journey will be well worth the effort. You are preparing for an adventure that can and will be transformational for you and your congregation.

In order for the journey to be successful, it is important to have a clear and compelling vision, to have willing and committed leadership, and to inspire people by creating a culture of gratitude, prayer, and faith. The fourth step in our C.L.I.M.B. acronym is *motivation*. How can we motivate others to pack their gear and come along up this mountain? How do we motivate people to join us in this journey of stewardship, to be imitators of God, to become more generous?

Ineffective Ways to Approach Stewardship

First, let's take a look at some of the appeals typically used in churches today. While well-intentioned, these appeals are occasionally successful in generating temporary boosts to the bottom line but are never successful in attaining the summit of effective and enduring stewardship.

1. Budget-driven Giving

In many of our churches today, the focus of the annual budget appeal is the operating budget itself. The church treasurer or finance chair informs the congregation that the utility costs are on the rise, insurance costs have skyrocketed, and the staff needs a cost-of-living adjustment. Programs, salaries, and overhead must be paid, so it is hoped that people will increase their giving. The message is, "Times are tough. Can you

God continues to express generosity and give to us in ways we can hardly imagine—not because of what we do, but because of grace. God's gifts come to us without strings attached. Our gifts to God should be returned in the same way.

please help us out?" For most of your church members, a plea to increase giving to satisfy increasing costs does little to inspire generosity. Spreadsheets and line-item budgets cause most people's eyes to glaze over, and they soon become distracted by thoughts of their own rising household expenses. While fiscal responsibility is important and the congregation must feel comfortable with the way in which finances are managed, your operating budget, and the need to fund it, does not assist people in reaching the summit of life-changing generosity. In fact, while a line-item budget is needed for accountability, it should never be a part of your stewardship process.

2. Fair-share Giving

Many congregations use an approach in which the amount needed to sustain current ministries is divided equally among families, resulting in a fair-share apportionment. Families are told what the church needs in order to fund programming, salaries, and overhead and what their portion of the total is. It is assumed that people want to contribute what is "owed" and that most will respond accordingly. This type of appeal is based on the concept of paying dues rather than anything inspirational (or, for that matter, spiritual). It is founded on the belief that people will feel obligated to pay for their portion of the church's budget. In some cases, people may feel they are not as financially able as others or are not using as many of the church's resources and, therefore, are not obligated to pay their "share." Others, who are in fact more financially able, may contribute only the portion requested of them. The result is an underfunded budget and an uninspired congregation.

3. Lottery, or "Giving-to-Get" Giving

The popularity of state lottery games has found its way into the lives of many of our congregations. For some, it is a misinterpretation of the Scripture from Luke 6:38: "Give, and it will be given to you. A good measure, pressed down, shaken together and running over, will be poured into your lap. For with the measure you use, it will be measured to you" (NIV). This passage has often been used to support the notion of "Give in order to get." We have even heard people provide testimonies indicating that once they chose to give away a greater portion of their earnings, soon they were given a promotion and salary increase. This type of thinking can lead us into a bartering relationship with God where we let God know we will give of ourselves and our resources but we expect God to reciprocate. Remember that God's blessings both preceded and exceeded any gift-giving on our

Certainly the congregation needs to know when a financial crisis has emerged; however, it is your vision for ministry that will encourage and inspire the congregation to resolve it.

part. God provided an abundance of blessings—indeed, all that we have and all that we are. God continues to express generosity and give to us in ways we can hardly imagine—not because of what we do, but because of grace. God's gifts come to us without strings attached. Our gifts to God should be returned in the same way. Consider the translation of Luke 6:37-38 from Eugene Peterson's *The Message*:

> Don't pick on people, jump on their failures, criticize their faults—unless, of course, you want the same treatment. Don't condemn those who are down; that hardness can boomerang. Be easy on people; you'll find life a lot easier. Give away your life; you'll find life given back, but not merely given back—given back with bonus and blessing. Giving, not getting, is the way. Generosity begets generosity.

This version's translation suggests that when you are generous, what is given back to you is life itself. Perhaps it is true that when one becomes more generous, a change in perspective occurs—a change in which life itself becomes a gift and gratitude is expressed. A grateful heart has no choice but to become generous.

4. Crisis Giving, or the Chicken Little Dance

Many times in our work, we have heard desperate pleas for funding. Often the church has found itself in some kind of financial bind due to economic changes in the community (for example, local factory closes), stock market decreases (for example, investment income no longer available to supplement other income), disruption to the church life (for example, embezzlement, internal feud, beloved clergy leaves), or another concern. Often this is handled by a cry for help from the church leadership insisting that if more income is not generated quickly, the church will need to fire staff or close its doors. In some cases, the circumstances may be quite bleak, but in many cases, the tragic nature of the church's financial affairs is inflated or at least prematurely stated. This cry for help not only inspires fear, but may lead people to believe the church is no longer viable. Henri Nouwen says, "When we seek to raise funds we are not saying, 'Please, could you help us out because lately it's been hard.' Rather, we are declaring, 'We have a vision that is amazing and exciting. We are inviting you to invest yourself through the resources that God has given you—your energy, your prayers, and your money—in this work to which God has called us.'"[2]

Certainly the congregation needs to know when a financial crisis has emerged; however, it is your vision for ministry that will encourage and inspire the congregation to resolve it.

> **"Why should I contribute?" is a much more important question than "How much should I contribute?"**

Remember to report your church's financial position with as much clarity as possible. Some churches report income and expenses by dividing them equally among twelve months, rather than prorating based on prior years' patterns. Many churches who use a calendar year as their fiscal year receive as much as 20 to 25 percent or more of income in December—the last month of the year. This type of reporting could lead your congregation to believe your income is trailing expenses for the entire year, only to discover there is a surplus after Christmas. Instead of telling your congregation, "The sky is falling," for eleven out of the twelve months of the year, share your budget clearly and provide frequent reminders about the important ministry it supports. Remember that people need to comprehend the connection between their generosity and your ability to accomplish ministry.

At this time, stop reading and reflect on the following questions:

1. Have you intentionally or unintentionally tried to motivate people to give in any of the four ways described above?

2. How has the congregation typically responded?

If the motivations discussed above are not the answer to achieving the summit of effective and enduring stewardship, then what is? What motivates people to contribute to your important ministries? How can you inspire them to higher levels of giving? Our experience has shown us time and again that people contribute in order to make a difference. People want to know that the funds they have given are not sitting idle but are being invested in ministries that are making a difference in the world and impacting people's lives. Church researcher George Barna said, "It is helpful to give evidence of the ministry needs people's money would be devoted to, show how efficiently the church uses money, demonstrate the life-changing impact of the church's ministry, and establish trust and confidence in the leadership of the church."[3] When members perceive that their contributions are being put into action and making a difference, they will be motivated to support your winning cause. This is the ideal primary motivation for your church members.

Communicating Your Message of Transformed Lives

As you plan your stewardship efforts and prepare to tell the compelling story of lives transformed through your ministries, it is important to connect people's contributions with your ability to do ministry. Many people make modest gifts to the church and never connect their giving with what is being accomplished. For people to be motivated to contribute more than a token gift, they need to hear how their gifts are being used to impact people's lives. In chapter 1 we discussed the fact that the question, Why should I contribute? is much more important than, How much should I contribute? Seeing and hearing stories of life-

When talking about your church's ministries, remember to limit facts and figures; instead, help people see the faces of those whose lives are changed forever because your members chose to contribute generously.

changing ministries answers the question why and motivates people to respond more generously, enabling you to successfully reach the summit. Your church is actively engaged in powerful ministry! Tell the story of how people's lives are made better because of the generous support of your members.

Here are some practical ways in which you can tell the story of your incredible ministries.

"Minutes for Mission" or "Did You Know?"

"Minutes for Mission" or "Did You Know?" moments are often used to share information with the congregation regarding the ministries funded by the annual budget. This time in front of your congregation can be a prime opportunity to connect member contributions with your ability to do ministry. Make the story as personal and powerful as possible—let people know how their generous support is having a direct impact on people's lives. Tell them how the transformative power of Jesus Christ has touched the lives of those whom you serve.

Oftentimes, people fall into the trap of reciting a history lesson rather than sharing their ministry story. Consider these two examples:

1. The pastor says, "Today we will hear from Betty Missioner, chair of the Outreach Committee, who is going to tell us about Habitat for Humanity." Betty says, "Good morning. I am pleased to be with you to tell you about an important ministry called Habitat for Humanity. Millard and Linda Fuller founded Habitat for Humanity International in 1976. Through the work of Habitat, thousands of low-income families have found new hope in the form of affordable housing. Churches, community groups, and others have joined together to successfully tackle a significant social problem—decent housing for all. Habitat for Humanity has built more than 300,000 houses, sheltering more than 1.5 million people in more than 3,000 communities worldwide. We hope you will give generously to this worthy cause."

While accurate and informative, this minute for mission does little to motivate giving. Consider this alternative:

2. The pastor says, "Today we will hear from Betty Missioner, chair of the Outreach Committee, who is going to tell us about Habitat for Humanity." Betty says, "Good morning. I am pleased to be with you to tell you about an organization that has provided

shelter and hope for more than 1.5 million people around the world. Let me tell you about just one of them. Alice Jones thought her days of raising children were over and had settled into a comfortable life of being a doting grandmother. She worked full-time as a nurse's assistant at the local hospital and had plenty of hobbies. Then one night, Alice's world came crashing down around her when her daughter was killed in a car accident. Overnight, Alice lost her daughter, and when her three grandchildren came to live with her, she began the task of raising children all over again. The small home in which she and several other relatives lived had plenty of room for her, but with the addition of her grandchildren, the quarters were exceedingly insufficient. Alice turned to Habitat for Humanity. An all-woman team came out to help her build her new home, and many of the nurses and doctors with whom Alice worked came out to help hammer nails as well.

"When Alice's home was dedicated, her three grandchildren danced with joy on the front lawn. She says she never thought she would be able to provide her grandchildren with the life they deserved after their mother passed away, but now in her new Habitat home, Alice says she finally feels as though she and her family are headed in the right direction.

"There are many more people just like Alice who deserve to have a decent home in which to live. Today, I hope you will help make that happen with a generous donation to Habitat for Humanity."

We don't pay the utility companies because we love paying utilities. We budget for utilities because of the many different ways in which the building is used for ministry.

Which story has a greater impact? Which story more clearly connects generous donations to the ability to influence lives? Remember to limit facts and figures; instead, help your congregation see the faces of those whose lives have been changed forever because your members chose to contribute generously.

One of our church clients had a Mechanics Ministry in which church members would repair cars to get them in good working condition and then donate them to a local family in need. One Sunday in worship, a recipient of one of the Mechanics Ministry's refurbished cars shared her story in a "Minute for Mission." Jane, a single mother with five children, had been unable to find secure employment since she had no transportation from her rural home to the city. Jane was forced to rely on food stamps and neighbors who would occasionally take her on errands. After receiving the refurbished car, Jane was able to find full-time employment and was no longer in need of public assistance. She and her family were hopeful about their future. Members of this congregation were able to see and hear firsthand how they were making an impact on people right in their community. Stories like this enable people to put faces on your ministries and will inspire generosity.

Cardboard Testimonies

The cardboard testimony is a simple but effective way to show your congregation the impact of the ministries in your church. On a piece of cardboard, invite people to write a brief phrase describing their lives before they became a part of your community of faith. On the reverse side, ask them to write how their lives have been transformed—how they are different as a result of your ministries. Some examples:

Side 1: Addicted to cocaine   Side 2: Addicted to God

Side 1: Death of our son   Side 2: New life in Christ

Side 1: Sideline Christian   Side 2: Going to be a missionary

This is a clear and profound way to show Christ's transformational love in the lives of your members. This is the kind of thing that needs to be seen and experienced to get the true impact. There are many examples available on www.youtube.com (search "cardboard testimonies"). Take a look.

The Budget Presentation

When you present your annual budget, keep in mind the various appeals we outlined earlier. Although people want to be assured that your leadership board is managing funds appropriately, very few of your members are eager to hear how you have minimized expenses by installing a more fuel-efficient furnace. Remember that when you tell people the church's expenses are going up, they are probably thinking how much their personal expenses are going up as well. While it is indeed true that your expenses are on the rise, just telling people will do little to motivate them to higher levels of generosity.

Remember that your operating budget is the resource that funds the building, staff, programs, and ministries. The budget exists simply as a means for ministry. For example, we don't pay the utility companies because we love paying utilities. We budget for utilities because of the many different ways in which the building is used for ministry. If you are like most congregations, your building is used throughout the week for 12-step groups, community groups, and your own programming. This requires heating and cooling, lighting, and insurance—all items included in your line-item budget. The important thing to recognize is that all the expenses included in your budget support the ministries you provide to your community. Without your staff, building, utilities, and other expenses, you would do little to build God's kingdom in your community. Your budget is much more than a list of revenues and expenses. Help your congregation appreciate it as a celebration of all the mission and ministry you are accomplishing.

 Ministry-focused Budget

One of the most effective methods of communicating your budget as ministry support is through a ministry-focused budget.

A ministry-focused budget is a powerful way to demonstrate the life-changing impact of the ministries your annual budget (members' contributions) supports. You are not replacing the line-item budget used by your finance committee, but merely restating it in a way that

You will need to consider the question, Now what? People want to know you have a plan for the future. If you are continuing to do what you have always done, why would people be compelled to give more?

enables people to see how much ministry is being accomplished through their giving.

To create the ministry-focused budget, look at your line-item budget and prorate each of the items into one of five ministry categories. Typically you will use (1) Worship, (2) Christian Education, (3) Communication, (4) Outreach, and (5) Pastoral Care. If you have another important ministry (for example, Music Ministry), you could include a sixth category (but please, never more than six). You should *not* separate administration or personnel as a category. In some churches, one of the most important elements of ministry support (and often the largest portion of the budget) is their clergy and staff. Your staff provides support to some or all of the five ministry categories. In your ministry-focused budget, the expenses associated with staff and building should reflect that support. For example, all expenses associated with your clergy should be divided among the five categories according to the amount of time devoted to each.

Imagine a church where the staff includes a senior minister, an associate minister, and a music minister. The senior minister's allocation may be 40 percent worship, 25 percent communications, 10 percent pastoral care, 5 percent outreach, and 20 percent Christian education. Much of the senior minister's time is devoted to preparing for worship and writing sermons. She or he is also responsible for new member assimilation (communications) and writes a weekly blog (communication). In addition, she teaches an ongoing adult Bible study class (Christian education) and makes some of the hospital visits (pastoral care). The associate pastor holds the majority of responsibilities for pastoral care, children and youth education, and organizes the annual mission trip. His or her allocation may be 10 percent worship, 30 percent pastoral care, 30 percent Christian education, 10 percent communications, and 20 percent outreach.

In terms of allocating overhead and building expenses, you may want to consider what percent of the week is devoted to worship, meetings held by church-affiliated groups, and meetings held by outside organizations (for example, 12-step groups and others). Remember, this is more of an art than a science—no sharpened pencils needed. Once you have divided your line-item budget among the five ministry categories, you will create a pie chart for each category. Each piece of the pie represents the percent of your budget that funds one of the five ministry categories. In a congregation where the total operating budget is $114,258, here is how the ministry-focused-budget pie chart would look:

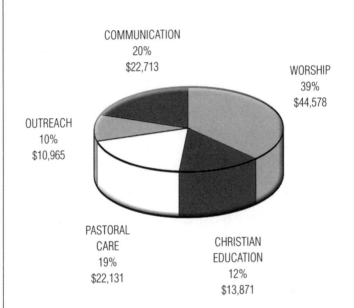

COMMUNICATION
20%
$22,713

WORSHIP
39%
$44,578

OUTREACH
10%
$10,965

PASTORAL
CARE
19%
$22,131

CHRISTIAN
EDUCATION
12%
$13,871

You don't want people to be enthused by the ministry that is happening but never make the connection between your congregation's ability to do ministry and their generosity.

Next you will create a page for each of the ministry areas. Each page should have plenty of white space, not too much verbiage, and lots of great photos. Tell your story succinctly and graphically. For example, on the Christian education page, tell about the programs you provide through your Christian education department. Show pictures of the participating kids, youth, and adults. Help people who have never participated in Christian education programs see what they have been missing. This is your opportunity to tell your story and celebrate your ministry. Use photos, quotations, and stories to help people see what great work you are accomplishing.

Last, you will need to consider the question, Now what? People want to know you have a plan for the future. If you are continuing to do what you have always done, why would people be compelled to give more? Go back to the conversations around your "clear and compelling vision" (chapter 1). What programs or projects emerged as a result of your discussions? What did you discover at the intersection of your strengths and the needs of your community? What is God's call to your faith community in this time and place? Let people know you have heard them. Tell them what you will do when resources become available. For example, if your people feel called to expand and diversify the music offerings in worship, tell them you plan to incorporate jazz music into a couple of the services next year. If you know how much it will cost, let people know. If one of your now-what items is to do more outreach, let people know how, whom, where, when, and how much. Do some homework and let people know you plan to take a group to Haiti to provide assistance to a medical mission. Let them know what resources will be necessary and, more important, what the result will be. This is your opportunity to help people see what it will look like when your congregation responds to God's call. Once you have created a ministry-focused budget, your congregation will want to see an update every year. In subsequent years, include a "We Did It!" section that lists all the items you accomplished the previous year. That lets your congregation members know you are doing what you said you would do with the gifts you have been given.

Along with the ministry-focused budget, there are several other ways to share your budget in terms of the ministries it supports.

Options for Presenting Your Budget as Ministry Support

A Ministry Fair

Invite each ministry area within your church to create a visual representation of the ministry they do. This does not mean just

However you choose to share the story of your ministries, keep in mind the picture you want to paint for your members—show them your church's vision for ministry. Help them see the significant difference your ministries are having on those whom you serve. Let them know what has been and will be accomplished because of the resources they have provided.

outreach groups, but includes any group that gathers for support, education, worship, prayer, fellowship, or outreach. Make sure your list is exhaustive. A tabletop display works well, or you may want to create a short video. Designate one Sunday as Ministry Fair Sunday. Each of your ministry areas should plan to have a display in your parish hall or other large space so people can walk around and learn more about what they do. You will need to publicize this well in advance and be sure to connect these ministries to the budget. You don't want people to be enthused by the ministry that is happening but never make the connection between your congregation's ability to do ministry and their generosity. A ministry fair is best held between or after worship services with light refreshments that travel well. To keep people in the building (rather than sneaking out the side door), consider renting a popcorn maker or hot-dog cooker. The smells will entice people to stay, and you will be guaranteed a captive audience.

Banner Procession

Particularly if your space does not permit a ministry fair, a "banner procession" can provide a similar effect. Invite each of the areas of ministry within the church to create a banner that represents who they are and how they are transforming lives in your community. Remember to tell the story in photos and phrases so people can quickly grasp the importance of each ministry. Hosting a banner-making workshop on a Saturday morning or Sunday afternoon excites people and inspires some friendly competition. Have your banner carriers line up and process into the sanctuary. As they are announced or enter, invite those who have been impacted by the ministry to stand up. Display your banners afterward around the church so people can take a closer look and become inspired.

PowerPoint Presentation

A fun and uplifting presentation depicting all the ministries in your congregation is also a great way to educate and encourage your people. Ask each of the ministry areas to provide a few good-quality photos and a few bullet points about their area of ministry. Create a brief (eight minutes or less) presentation that conveys the incredible ministry that is happening in and through your church. Stream your presentation to your website, make copies on CDs, and mail them to your list of members and friends. If you have the right equipment, you can show this during worship or in a special adult forum. It is often a good idea to also create a trifold brochure that lists the various ministry groups, the names of contact people, and a couple of sentences about what each group does and whom they help. This will also give someone who wants to get involved the ability to do so. If possible, combine this with a minute-for-mission presentation— the impact will be powerful!

Using Other Means for Communication

You have many communication vehicles at your disposal, including websites, bulletins, newsletters (electronic and paper), and e-mail. Be sure to use them all. Tell your community how you are fulfilling God's vision and why this vision is worthy of their support. Keep in mind that some of your families may be quite generous, but their generosity is expressed through their giving to other charities. Many not-for-profit organizations are communicating with your members and telling their stories well. Be sure you are just as diligent. You may want to include a regular column in your newsletter on stewardship topics including Scripture passages, quotes, and devotions. You can also use these vehicles to educate your members on current levels of giving in your congregation. Providing a pie chart that demonstrates the current levels of giving from your households is typically an eye-opener. Remember, this chart is intended to provide information only and should not include commentary or judgment. Help everyone stay informed by utilizing all the communication tools at your disposal.

However you choose to share the story of your ministries, keep in mind the picture you want to paint for your members—show them your church's vision for ministry. Help them see the significant difference your ministries are having on those whom you serve. Let them know what has been and will be accomplished because of the resources they have provided. Remember, people are motivated to give when they envision the powerful impact of their generosity on the lives of others. Help your church family see the power of your ministries and they will rise to levels of generosity greater than even they had imagined as they approach the summit of enduring and effective stewardship.

CHAPTER FIVE

Boldly Ask

Even veteran mountain climbers, who have trained and prepared well, can get turned away at one of the most challenging points in the climb to Everest's summit—Hillary's Step. According to PBS, "The most famous physical feature on Everest, the Hillary Step, at 28,750 feet, is a 40-foot spur of snow and ice. First climbed in 1953 by Edmund Hillary and Tenzing Norgay, the Hillary Step is the last obstacle barring access to the gently angled summit slopes."[1] What is your obstacle in reaching the summit of transformational stewardship? Hopefully you have successfully shared your compelling vision for ministry, raised up competent leaders, sought God's inspiration, and motivated your congregation through mission and ministry. The next step, to boldly ask, is the last hurdle as you seek to attain the summit of transformational stewardship.

As you consider this last significant step in the process, bear in mind the words from James 4:2: "You do not have, because you

If you truly believe in your clear and compelling vision, why would you *not* invite others to join you in fulfilling it? If you truly believe you are being called by God to accomplish your ministry objectives, how could you *not* encourage others to get on board?

do not ask." How often does a church discover a major giver in their midst while reading an article in the local newspaper about the person's gift to the local hospital or university? Why is the hospital the gift recipient instead of the church? More often than not, it is because the hospital asked and the church did not.

How you invite people to participate in giving conveys volumes about the importance of the gift to the ministries of your church. If you truly believe in your clear and compelling vision, why would you *not* invite others to join you in fulfilling it? If you truly believe you are being called by God to accomplish your ministry objectives, how could you *not* encourage others to get on board? Remember the little church that said they couldn't invite people because their pews were already overcrowded? What they failed to recognize was that they had the answer to a world that is broken and hurting. If they truly believed theirs was a church where people could find the grace, love, and hope of Jesus Christ, they would not have been able to contain themselves. They would have been overcome with enthusiasm for inviting others to join them and would have dared to ask boldly.

Without intentional follow-up, you communicate a lack of urgency and diminish the importance of the members' pledges. A sense of urgency must be a part of your communication.

Consider this example of how one congregation chose to ask for members' support. At the first meeting of the St. Swithin's stewardship committee, one person expressed her opinion that there was no need to do a "big" campaign. She felt people would give what they could, so asking boldly was unnecessary. The committee decided to simply mail out pledge cards with a brief note from the church treasurer indicating an increase in church expenses of 10 percent over the last year. A month after the mailing, when the stewardship committee reconvened, they were discouraged to discover only 50 percent of the pledging families had returned the cards. A veteran of the stewardship committee remarked, "People always take a long time to return their pledge cards. In fact, we can count on some families to turn them in as late as March of next year." As predicted, the trickle of pledge cards continued, with the last ones received in early March. The results—an overall 15 percent decrease in pledges. So what went wrong?

> We are dedicating our financial resources—often the most difficult to surrender—to further God's kingdom. A procession of faithful members bringing their pledges forward and placing them on God's altar is an outward and visible sign of commitment and discipleship.

Considering the many elements of the "ask" or invitation to give, here are a few observations:

1. In the previous scenario, pledge cards are simply sent out in the mail—a very transactional and impersonal approach. The person completes the pledge card either alone or with a family member, and mails or hand-carries it to the church. This process is similar to responding to a bill or an invoice and does nothing to convey the spiritual aspects of transformational stewardship.

2. The letter with the pledge card refers to the church's increase in expenses, but says nothing about the exciting ministry initiatives that will be launched next year. The letter fails to answer the question, Why should I support this church by giving my hard-earned dollars? A person may ask (and rightfully so), "If the church leadership plans to do only the same things it did last year, why should I contribute more? My expenses are going up too!"

3. Having chosen only one method of asking (that is, the pledge card), it is likely St. Swithin's has missed the mark, particularly with younger generations. Younger folks, and more and more older members, are likely to prefer making pledges and gifts electronically through transfer of funds, credit or debit cards, and other more modern but perhaps as-yet nontraditional ways. Generally, for younger members, the importance of making a pledge and, for that matter, passing the plate, has less significance than it had for the older generations.

4. In the previous example, pledges are allowed to linger for months and months without any follow-up from leadership. The statement from the veteran stewardship committee member that some families wait until March to return their cards becomes a self-fulfilling prophecy. Without intentional follow-up, you communicate a lack of urgency and diminish the importance of the members' pledges. You have a compelling vision that God has placed in front of you. Your ministry objectives are bold and transformational! A sense of urgency must be a part of your communication.

At this time, stop reading and reflect on the following questions:

1. Considering your previous stewardship efforts, do you feel you have "boldly asked"?

2. How has your communication to the congregation conveyed the importance and urgency of your ministry objectives?

Remember that Jesus never spoke of tithing. In fact, he asked the rich young ruler to give it all! Not 10 percent—all of it!

Let's take each element of the ask and offer some alternatives that may just put you over the top of the transformational stewardship summit:

1. When and How the Ask Is Made

We believe the stewardship journey is grounded in gratitude, revealed in prayer, and lived in faith. So making a pledge, a promise to return to God a portion of the gifts you have been given, is a worshipful act. Therefore, we encourage churches to distribute and complete pledge cards as an act of worship within the context of the worship services rather than mailing out the pledge cards. For many of the churches with whom we work, this initially sounds a bit scary, and they are hesitant to try it. Concerns raised include, "What if someone looks over my shoulder and sees what I am giving?" and "What about those who do not wish to make a pledge or those who are still praying about it?" These are good questions and need to be addressed. If people are serious about inviting God into the process of determining the amount of their pledge, and if they are convinced they are following God's will for their giving, why would they be concerned about someone looking over their shoulder to see the amount of the pledge they are making? In other words, if God and I have talked it over and I feel I am complying with God's will, why would I worry about what anyone else thinks? For those who are making a zero pledge or are still praying, this can simply be noted on the pledge card and turned in. Everyone who is in worship on the day pledge cards are completed should be able to make an appropriate response on their card.

Once they give it a try, most churches discover that one of the most meaningful elements of their campaigns is when members leave their pews or chairs and bring their pledge cards forward and place them on the altar. The symbolism contained in this act is powerful and profound. We are dedicating our financial resources—often the most difficult to surrender—to further God's kingdom. A procession of faithful members bringing their pledges forward and placing them on God's altar is an outward and visible sign of commitment and discipleship.

2. Meeting People Where They Are

Meeting people where they are on their journey to the summit may require a variety of "asks" instead of simply mailing out a pledge card and waiting for them to come back. For those who are tithing, it is likely they have already discovered the joy of generosity and may well have achieved the summit of transformational stewardship. Therefore, their giving is likely to continue to increase. However, that is not to say all their giving will be directed toward your church. Be sure to affirm their choice in giving to your church by letting them know how funds are being used to accomplish your ministry objectives. Remember that Jesus never spoke of tithing. In fact, he asked the rich young ruler to give it all! Not 10 percent—all of it! Through our experiences, we have often encountered people who are so caught up in the joy of generosity that giving away 10 percent is no longer sufficient. One pastor had a personal goal of giving 50 percent of his income away. Another layperson witnessed to giving away 30 percent of her income with a goal of giving away 90 percent and living on just 10 percent. These generous givers have surely found themselves at the summit of transformational stewardship. Make sure you invite them to share their stories so others may learn from their experiences on the journey.

For those who are new in faith or have grown accustomed to low-level giving, inviting them to tithe will probably not be effective. For someone who is giving less than 5 percent of his or her income, the idea of tithing can be daunting, to say the least. We have seen many churches incorporate the message of growing 1 percent of income per year until the tithe has been reached. We have also seen churches invite members to try out the tithe for a period of time, such as three months or so. Both these methods work well with those who are stuck at "base camp" and are having difficulty envisioning the summit. Another approach is to suggest members compare what they are currently giving to the church with what they are spending in other areas of their lives. For instance, you might suggest that members consider how their gifts to the church compare to what they pay for cell phone service, soccer lessons, or country club dues. Help them begin to look at their checkbooks as barometers of their faith. Remember, Jesus said, "Where your treasure is, there your heart will be also" (Matthew 6:21). What does it say about what we value if we contribute $300 to the ministries of the church and spend $1,000 per year on Starbucks coffee? How we choose to distribute the financial (and other) resources God has provided says much about what we value. Help those who are newer in faith make this connection.

3. Generational Differences

Gone are the days when people attended worship weekly and gave generously out of a sense of obligation. The generations of people born before 1946, Builders (born 1901–1924) and Silents (born 1925–1945), believe strongly in civic and religious causes. Influenced by the World Wars and the Great Depression, these folks are primarily responsible for the growth of mainline denominations and local churches, as well as civic groups such as Rotary and Kiwanis. The members of these generations are much more likely to make gifts regardless of who the preacher is, how dynamic the worship service is, or how vital the church's ministries are. They give because they perceive it as the right thing to do. That's not to say Builders and Silents are uninterested in the impact of the church's ministries on those whom you serve. They can be motivated to extreme generosity when the vision for

God's call to your church is clear, compelling, and urgent! There are people right outside your doors who do not yet know about the good news of Jesus Christ. God is calling you to powerful ministry, and you need the resources God has provided through your members to accomplish it.

ministry is clear and the impact on lives is great.

As these faithful servants age and pass away, the leadership in local churches has shifted to those born 1946 and later known as the Baby Boomers and Gen Xers. Generationally, the people born 1946 and later grew up without an inherent sense of loyalty and commitment, particularly to the local church. In fact, Baby Boomers (born 1946 to 1964) attend church much less frequently and tend to view giving as a type of investment. Boomers want to know what they are getting in return for their gift. In other words, what type of an impact will my gift make on the lives of those whom we serve? Can I make a gift elsewhere that will provide a bigger bang for the buck? Baby Boomers are also much more likely to make designated gifts and request the use of credit cards for giving (they are interested in receiving frequent-flier miles or reward points for their purchases). We'll address the topic of online giving and other ways to give in a moment, but the bottom line is if you can offer a list of giving opportunities that is specific and concrete, you are likely to get a Baby Boomer to make a gift. It will be important, however, that you follow up to let the Boomer know how the gift was put to good use. Boomers need to hear that their gift was put to the intended use and that it had the anticipated impact.

So what about those born after 1964? The full impact of Gen Xers (born 1965–1981) and Millennials (born 1982–2003) on churches today has not yet been determined. Gen Xers and Millennials are much less likely than their elders to feel a sense of affiliation with any particular denomination. They also attend worship more sporadically than earlier generations.[2] Gen Xers tend to think more skeptically when processing information, so be sure your messages to them are authentic and direct. They also will likely be repelled by overly slick communications that may be perceived as disingenuous. While many Millennials are still working their way to adulthood, early indications are they will follow the path of Gen Xers when it comes to church affiliations. A study by the Barna Group demonstrated that Millennials are more skeptical and resistant to Christianity than people of the same age only a decade ago.[3] However, most Millennials have been raised with a sense of duty to give back to their communities through volunteerism. In fact, many Millennials are required to log volunteer hours as a high school graduation requirement. While Millennials may be more difficult to reach during worship services (due to irregular attendance), electronic communications, including e-mail and texting, are important vehicles to include in your overall communications strategy. Regardless of generation or delivery method, the message of lives transformed as a result of your active ministries is still the most powerful motivator.

4. Communicating the Urgency and Importance of Each Member's Contribution

If the approach is timid and the pledge card is simply mailed out in the hopes it may find its way back to the church, what does this convey about the importance of the member's contribution? If pledge cards are sent out to nonresponders and no one ever follows up, how important must the members' response be? God's call to your church is clear, compelling, and urgent! There are people right outside your doors who do not yet know about the good news of Jesus Christ. God is calling you to powerful ministry, and you need the resources God has provided through your members to accomplish it. Phone calls should be made to every active household (giving and/or attending) in your congregation no more than one week after you have received pledges in worship. Making follow-up phone calls sets expectations. People realize they are expected to make a response, even if they do not make a pledge. It is not the size of the gift that matters, but the prayerful and faithful nature with which the gift was determined. Choosing not to make phone calls says the member's pledge is not important. If you linger for several weeks before making phone calls, you have conveyed a lack of urgency.

There is ministry to be done right now! Don't we tend to deal with high-priority items first? Expression of your stewardship and the

An expeditious and heartfelt thank-you to your givers is one of the most important activities you can do to ensure a subsequent gift.

ability to fund your important ministries should be high priority and treated as such. So don't delay. Make the calls. You will be glad you did. A sample timeline, script for callers, and example letter can be found in appendix F. Make sure you follow up with nonresponders as quickly and effectively as possible.

5. Year-Round Giving

For some, the pledge they make is what they intend to contribute, but for others, their pledge may not reflect the entirety of their ability or willingness to contribute. There are several ways to encourage additional contributions above the amount pledged as well as ensure you will receive a substantial pledge from the member again the next year. First, because different types of giving opportunities appeal to different people, you must offer a variety of options for giving year-round. Pledging is the most common, but for some this is not a familiar or comfortable practice. The challenge is to make the variety of options as accessible and well-known as pledging. For example,

> To boldly ask is to firmly plant one's flag on the summit of transformative stewardship. To boldly ask invites people to join us on the summit and experience the transformation that comes through a life of giving, discipleship, and generosity.

several large churches have installed giving kiosks in their main entrances and gathering spaces. Granger Community Church of Granger, Indiana, has several kiosks clearly marked where you can swipe your credit or debit card and make a gift. The process resembles an ATM transaction and is quite familiar to most people. Lovers Lane United Methodist Church in Dallas uses giving kiosks as well as other options such as eChecks and online giving via credit or debit card. Some members of your congregation may balk at the idea of a giving kiosk or even giving online. However, it is important to provide a variety of giving opportunities and ways in which to contribute. This will ensure high levels of participation and enable you to accomplish your important ministry objectives. One size does not fit all when it comes to ways in which to make a contribution and express our gratitude to God.

Another way to encourage additional gifts above and beyond the pledge is to offer the opportunity to make a capital and/or planned gift. Typically, annual giving comes from a person's annual income or salary. Others, especially those who live on investment income, may be willing and able to provide financial support to a capital campaign or endowment fund. A capital campaign allows donors to make a substantial gift, in addition to their annual gift, for the purposes of a particular project or ministry focus. For those who are retired, the opportunity to participate in a planned giving program may allow them to make a gift in perpetuity that would have been impossible for them during their lifetimes. Many churches with whom we have worked express an interest in generating more planned gifts. There are many planned giving tools that are fairly easy and straightforward. For example, a church member might (1) consider a charitable gift annuity where the member (or their designee) earns a fixed rate of interest for life. Upon death, the annuity is donated to the church. This not only allows the member to support the church he or she loves *and* create a steady stream of income for life, but also provides a tax deduction in the year it is created; (2) donate a paid-up life insurance policy to the church; (3) make the church a beneficiary (or one of the beneficiaries) of a 401(k) or IRA; or (4) remember to include the church in their will or estate plans. Providing a multitude of giving choices allows your members to express their stewardship in ways that are meaningful and significant to them.

6. Saying Thank You

What does it convey to your church members if you receive a gift or pledge and never acknowledge its receipt and never express your thanks? What if that thank-you arrives months after the gift has been made? An expeditious and heartfelt thank-you to your givers is one of the most important activities you can do to ensure a subsequent gift. Acknowledge pledges as soon as possible, preferably within a week of their receipt, and express gratitude to those who enable you to move forward in mission and ministry. Send statements, at least quarterly, to all givers of record, expressing thanks and affirming how their gifts are being used to affect lives and how their next gift will help you do the same. Eliminate those boxed envelopes that are too small to send in the U.S. mail. Instead, send quarterly statements that (1) inform givers of the contributions they have made, (2) thank them for their generosity, (3) tell them how their gifts are being put to good use, (4) tell them how their next gift will also be put to good use, (5) provide self-addressed, mailable envelopes (one per month = three per quarterly statement) that can be used to send a check if they will not be in worship. Be sure to also provide information about how to make a gift online through your website or through their own financial institution.

At this time, stop reading and reflect on the following questions:

1. In a given year, how many opportunities are members offered to express their stewardship?

2. What can you do to better communicate your compelling vision for ministry across generational lines?

3. How have you been thanking those who support your ministries? How can you find ways to thank them more quickly and more often?

For those of you who boldly ask for your members' support, not only will you have demonstrated the importance of each member's contribution, but you will have expressed the urgency in accomplishing your important ministries.

As an experiment in boldly asking, we once encouraged a group to try tithing for a three-month period of time. After praying about whether God was calling them to this challenge of consistent tithing, some first-timers were brave enough to make this leap of faith. Most of those who took the plunge were giving between 2 percent and 3 percent of their incomes and were now preparing to give away 10 percent. After the three-month period, participants were asked to provide some reflections on their experience. Here are a few:

- "Amazingly—and I truly mean this—amazingly, there was always enough. It did make me more aware of how I was spending. I acknowledged that I was spending more frivolously than I had thought and reined some of that in to be able to meet the tithe."
- "We felt good about what we were doing. It was fun to calculate each week as our income fluctuated. It was very meaningful to support a new mission, which we wouldn't have had we not started tithing."
- "It did feel different writing a check each pay period for 10 percent of my pay. It felt more significant to me."
- "I was amazed to find that I could afford to live comfortably and that God provides—and all that is necessary is always there."

- "I always thought tithers were on the extreme end of things. So either I've changed my opinion or now I'm extreme."
- "I feel it enables me to trust God more, and it has strengthened my faith."

Not exactly what you might expect from people who suddenly began giving away three or more times what they had been giving previously. Maybe that's why ex-tithers are in such short supply.

In many ways, to boldly ask is to firmly plant one's flag on the summit of transformative stewardship. To boldly ask invites people to join us on the summit and experience the transformation that comes through a life of giving, discipleship, and generosity.

Conclusion

As you prepare for your ascent to the summit of transformational stewardship, keep in mind the story of the golden Buddha from chapter 3. This analogy not only holds true for us as individuals but also applies to the church. Just like the golden Buddha, the church is a golden treasure that has been covered with layers and layers of mud. As we meet with churches all over the country, we discover many that are mired in the mud of shrinking budgets, declining attendance, diminished giving, and the fear of scarcity.

One of the tragedies of the story of the Buddha is that when the village was invaded, all the monks were killed. Because no one was left who knew the truth about the mud-covered Buddha, it was left abandoned. No one was left to tell the story of the vast treasure that lay beneath the surface.

In our work with churches, it appears many have forgotten the treasure that lies beneath the surface—the good news of God's love and generosity. They have no one left to tell the story. Lives are still being changed, but for some reason people don't or won't tell the story. One mainline church caught in the cycle of declining attendance and fewer dollars fought long and hard against the idea of letting people tell their stories. After all, we might make someone else "feel bad" because God didn't do that for them. How sad! Ultimately, C.L.I.M.B. is about chipping away at the mud that has covered our churches for far too long to reveal the sacred treasure of God's steadfast love and abundant generosity, and the resulting transformed lives.

As you relate your compelling vision of changed lives; as your leadership passionately shares that vision; as you become inspired through gratitude, prayer, and faith; as you are motivated through ministry and mission; as you learn to ask boldly for support, slowly the mud begins to fall away, and God's golden treasure will be revealed for all the world to see. May your journey to the summit be so extraordinary that all will see the hand of God.

APPENDIX A

Scripture and Themes for Vision and Mission

Genesis 12; 15

God gave a vision to Abram, not a vision of bricks and mortar, but a vision of being a blessing to all people, a vision of influencing the world for God. In the midst of Abram's fear and wondering if it would ever happen, God took Abram outside to affirm the vision and told him to count the stars, if he was able, and that would be the number of his descendants. Whatever your project is, connect it to the countless stars in the sky, the countless unnamed lives that will be forever changed because of what you do in this campaign. It's not about bricks and mortar; go outside and count the stars!

Genesis 32:24-30

God had plans for Jacob, but Jacob wasn't too sure about the whole thing. In the midst of God's vision for Jacob, he had to wrestle with God and wrestle with his own lack of trust. In the end the blessing came as a result of struggle. And because of Jacob's willingness to struggle, the world was forever changed. You have struggled, you have wrestled with God and yourselves, but now you are ready to move forward. And yes, you believe that because of what you do, the world will be forever changed.

Exodus 35–36

A bunch of slaves gathered in the desert, so poor they didn't even have the straw to make bricks when they were back in Egypt, and yet they were commanded by God to build a tabernacle of precious skins and stones. It didn't make any sense. They believed that this was what God desired. "Everyone whose heart was stirred" (Exodus 35:21) came and made their offering. And somehow the impossible became possible, but it all began with the belief that this was what God wanted. It's not a project of the board, the pastor, or a few key laypeople. Believe that this vision is ultimately God's vision.

Mark 2:1-12

Any of the healing stories can be utilized in wonderful ways to talk about the mission and ministry of the church. What you are about is not bricks and mortar but creating a place where people can come to meet the healing presence of God's love and grace. And when people really believe that *Yes, this is what we are about*, then they are willing to go to absurd lengths to help make it happen. In this Scripture passage, the four friends had a vision of their friend healed and whole, and then they set about to make it happen.

Luke 9:46-48

Renovations and buildings are not about your own comfort but about creating a place where people are welcomed and made to feel at home. In the midst of talking about greatness, Jesus placed a child on his lap and said that true greatness was not about size, not about bricks and mortar, but about welcoming the child.

Leadership Resources on Vision and Mission

Drucker, Peter F., et al. *The Five Most Important Questions You Will Ever Ask About Your Organization*. San Francisco: Jossey-Bass, 2008.

Mancini, Will. *Church Unique: How Missional Leaders Cast Vision, Capture Culture, and Create Movement*. Leadership Network Series. San Francisco: Jossey-Bass, 2008.

McNeal, Reggie. *Missional Renaissance: Changing the Scorecard for the Church*. Leadership Network Series. San Francisco: Jossey-Bass, 2009.

Oswald, Roy M. *Discerning Your Congregation's Future: A Strategic and Spiritual Approach*. Herndon, Va.: Alban Institute, 1996.

Rendle, Gil, and Alice Mann. *Holy Conversations: Strategic Planning as a Spiritual Practice for Congregations.* Herndon, Va.: Alban Institute, 2003.

Rivers, Robert S. *From Maintenance to Mission: Evangelization and the Revitalization of the Parish.* Mahwah, N.J: Paulist Press, 2005.

Oldies but Goodies

Barna, George. *The Power of Vision: Discover and Apply God's Plan for Your Life and Ministry.* Ventura, Calif.: Regal, 1992.

Callahan, Kennon. *Twelve Keys to an Effective Church: Strong, Healthy Congregations Living in the Grace of God.* 2nd ed. San Francisco: Jossey-Bass, 2009.

Warren, Rick. *The Purpose Driven Church: Growth Without Compromising Your Message and Mission.* Grand Rapids: Zondervan, 1995.

APPENDIX C

Resources for Stewardship Education of Leadership

Books

Burk, Penelope. *Donor-Centered Fundraising*. Chicago, Ill.: Cygnus Applied Research, 2003.

Christopher, J. Clif. *Not Your Parents' Offering Plate: A New Vision for Financial Stewardship*. Nashville: Abingdon Press, 2008.

Durall, Michael. *Creating Congregations of Generous People*. Herndon, Va.: Alban Institute, 1999.

Jeavons, Thomas H., and Rebekah Burch Basinger. *Growing Givers' Hearts: Treating Fundraising as Ministry*. San Francisco: Jossey-Bass, 2000.

MacNaughton, John H. *More Blessed to Give: Straight Talk on Stewardship*. Harrisburg, Pa.: Church Publishing, 2002.

McSwain, Stephen. *The Giving Myths: Giving Then Getting the Life You've Always Wanted*. Macon, Ga.: Smyth and Helwys, 2007.

Nouwen, Henri J. M. *A Spirituality of Fundraising*. Edited by John S. Mogabgab. Nashville: Upper Room, 2010.

Powell, Mark Allan. *Giving to God: The Bible's Good News about Living a Generous Life*. Grand Rapids: Eerdmans, 2006.

Westerhoff, John H. *Grateful and Generous Hearts*. Harrisburg, Pa.: Morehouse, 2002.

Other Resources

Crown Financial Ministries: www.crown.org

Ecumenical Stewardship Center: www.stewardshipresources.org

Episcopal Network for Stewardship: www.tens.org

Evangelical Lutheran Church in America: www.elca.org/Growing-In-Faith/Discipleship/Stewardship.aspx

Generous Giving: www.generousgiving.org

Nooma (DVDs): www.nooma.com

Stewardship of Life: www.stewardshipoflife.org

Stewardship Statement Examples

The Stewardship Statement is a document that helps church leadership and the congregation articulate their beliefs around stewardship. It is typically helpful to have a section of statements describing what "we believe" followed by a section describing what "we commit ourselves to." The concluding paragraph should include an invitation to the congregation to adhere to the beliefs outlined in the Stewardship Statement.

Example 1

WE BELIEVE in a generous, loving, and self-giving God.
WE BELIEVE:

- All that we are and all that we have comes from God.
- God has been generous to us so that we can be generous to others.
- We are a society that is challenged by an addictive, self-destructive relationship with money and possessions.
- Christ longs to set us free from this bondage and restore us to life-giving relationships with God, one another, and all creation.

WE COMMIT OURSELVES TO:

- Staying close to Jesus, who is the one who revitalizes and transforms us.
- Discerning God's will for our lives through the holy habits of daily prayer, study, weekly worship, observing the Sabbath, tithing, and other intentional spiritual practices.
- Living enthusiastically, sharing ourselves (all that we are) and our gifts from God (all that we have) to be instruments of God's reconciling love in the world.
- Giving to God the *first* portion of our time, talent, money, and all our resources—not merely the leftovers.

WE PLEDGE OURSELVES to dare to imagine, initiate, and create personal and corporate ministries that can be outward and visible signs of God's kingdom on earth.

WE INVITE our parish family to join us in this lifelong, joyful, transforming, and liberating response to God's call to us.

(Adapted from Standing Commission on Stewardship and Development, *Report to the 75th General Episcopal Convention*.)

Example 2

Stewardship Statement
The Vestry, Clergy, and Stewardship Committee of St.
Swithin's Episcopal Church

WE BELIEVE we are created in the image of a generous, loving, and self-giving God.

WE BELIEVE:

• All that we are, all that we have, and all that we need comes from God.

• God calls us to be generous and loving.

• We are called to celebrate God's blessings by giving joyfully.

WE COMMIT TO:

• Giving to God the first portion of our time, talent, money, and all our resources—not merely the leftovers.

• Nurturing an ever-deepening spiritual relationship with God.

• Tithing or working intentionally toward tithing.

WE INVITE YOU TO:

• Open your heart to experience the joy of giving.

• Dare to imagine a stronger connection with God that manifests itself in a growing ministry to and for one another and the world.

• Join the Vestry, Clergy, and Stewardship Committee of St. Swithin's by signing this statement.

Ministry-Focused Budget

The purpose of the ministry-focused budget is to translate money into ministry. Your members want to know how their gifts to your church are being put to good use. What ministry is taking place, and how are people's lives better because of their contributions? This is a tool to answer those questions. It is also an opportunity to share with your congregation what your vision is for the coming year. Tell people how their gifts have been put to good use—then tell them how their next gift will be used to fulfill God's vision for your ministry.

Example

This example is to be printed on 11 x 17 paper, made into a booklet by folding it in half. By folding the paper in half again, it can be made into a self-mailer so no envelope is required. The number of pages is somewhat dependent on how you space things out. You will need to look at your operating expenses and divide them among at least five (no more than six) ministry categories. We recommend using (1) Christian Education, (2) Communication, (3) Outreach, (4) Pastoral Care, and (5) Worship. This means you will *not* have a salaries or administrative costs category. These expenses are ministry support. Divide them equitably among your ministry categories.

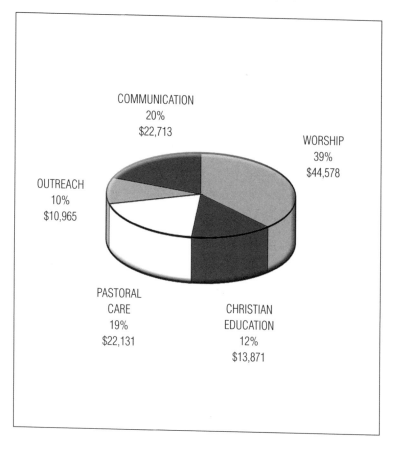

Here's how you might lay out your pages:

Page 1(Cover)   Your theme for the year and/or a Scripture reference.

Page 2   What is your vision for ministry? What are you doing next year that you did not do last year?

Page 3   A letter from your pastor, including photo.

Page 4   Christian Education: Highlight the programs and activities that are a part of your Christian education program. Use lots of photos and a few bullet points. Identify what percent of your operating expenses is enabling these activities to take place. Last, tell your members what you will do next when resources become available.

Page 5   Communications

Page 6   Pastoral Care

Page 7   Outreach

Page 8   Worship

Additional pages (optional):

• Include a letter from your leadership board and/or stewardship committee.

• Include your Stewardship Statement.

• Include a pie chart depicting your members' current levels of giving. In this chart, there are two households giving $15,000 or more annually, four households giving $10,000–$14,999 annually, and so on. Calculate what percent of income your median giver is contributing based on area demographics. How much would be available for ministry if all giving households chose to contribute 5 percent or 10 percent of income to the church? (Caution: Presentation of this chart to the congregation can stir a lot of discussion, especially regarding those who are giving the most and those who are giving the least. Most of this discussion is healthy and helpful, but you should be prepared to respond to questions and concerns raised.)

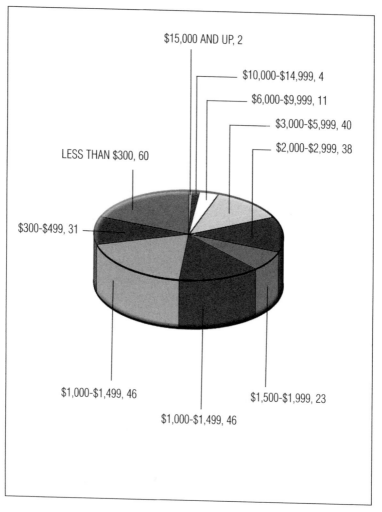

$15,000 AND UP, 2

$10,000-$14,999, 4

$6,000-$9,999, 11

$3,000-$5,999, 40

$2,000-$2,999, 38

LESS THAN $300, 60

$300-$499, 31

$1,000-$1,499, 46

$1,000-$1,499, 46

$1,500-$1,999, 23

- Provide a reflection on a stewardship Scripture.
- Discuss tithing and/or proportional giving.
- Provide a proportional giving table using income levels appropriate to your membership. Make sure 10 percent is not the highest category.

ANNUAL INCOME	2%	4%	6%	8%	10%	12%	15%
$30,000	$600	$1,200	$1,800	$2,400	$3,000	$3,600	$4,500
$40,000	$800	$1,600	$2,400	$3,200	$4,000	$4,800	$6,000
$50,000	$1,000	$2,000	$3,000	$4,000	$5,000	$6,000	$7,500
$75,000	$1,500	$3,000	$4,500	$6,000	$7,500	$9,000	$11,250
$100,000	$2,000	$4,000	$6,000	$8,000	$10,000	$12,000	$15,000
$125,000	$2,500	$5,000	$7,500	$10,000	$12,500	$15,000	$18,750
$150,000	$3,000	$6,000	$9,000	$12,000	$15,000	$18,000	$22,500
$175,000	$3,500	$7,000	$10,500	$14,000	$17,500	$21,000	$26,250

• If you receive income from a source other than pledges, include a pie chart showing what the sources are and how much income they provide.

Do not skimp on this publication or cut corners. Use color, at least for the cover, and high-resolution photos. Make sure you mail this to every congregation member's household and keep some extra copies on hand for visitors.

APPENDIX F

Making Contact

1. Letter to Those Who Have Pledged

On the day after you have received pledges in worship (or as soon after as possible), send a letter similar to the one below to all members. Include a self-addressed envelope (#9) without a stamp and a blank pledge card.

As you know, our Commitment Service was yesterday. It was an inspiring and exciting time as those present made commitments to support the ministries of St. Swithin's for 2012. The enthusiasm that God has generated has been contagious! So far, [number] households have committed [$total dollar amount] in support of the vision for our church.

To enable God's vision for our church to become a reality, we invite you to join the many others who have made their commitments. There are two ways to do so.

First, you will find enclosed a pledge card. You may fill it out and return it in the envelope provided or place it in the offering plate on Sunday. Please be sure to include a total amount so that we do not misunderstand your wishes. Even if you do not feel led to contribute financially at this time, please return the card and indicate a "$0" pledge. This way, we will know your intentions.

Second, if you prefer a personal conversation with a member of our campaign team, you may simply hold your card until we contact you. Our commitment team will be making personal contacts between (date) and (date).

If your pledge card has crossed with this letter in the mail, thank you for your faithfulness.

We are delighted and thankful that you are a member of our church family, and we look forward to sharing in ministry together. May Christ continue to bless you and all disciples in our congregation.

Sincerely,

[campaign directors]

2. Preparing the List for Callers

This is a tool you can use to prepare those who will be making phone calls to those who have not yet made a pledge. These contacts should be made only to those persons who have previously made a commitment to your operating budget. Remember that your ministry needs are urgent, and every pledge is important in helping your church achieve God's vision. As such, these calls should be made no more than ten days after Commitment Sunday.

1. Print a set of labels for nonresponding households (only those who have previously made a gift to the church)—include first and last names, addresses, and home phone numbers. Affix labels to index cards.

2. Divide index cards among callers. Each caller should receive no more than ten cards.

3. Callers should pray before each phone call and be prepared to share their enthusiasm about this time in the life of your church and the fact that they have already made a pledge.

4. Callers are not to pressure or sell. The caller's job is to invite participation and bring closure to the pledge process. This is not a time to cajole or argue.

5. Callers should encourage people to return their pledge cards by the following Sunday if possible.

6. Callers should record responses on their index cards. If in the process of calling a pastoral concern is discovered, ask if you may share this information with your pastor.

7. When calls are completed, callers should return index cards to the stewardship chair.

8. If someone needs a pledge card, please notify the church office or offer to complete the card for the person over the phone.

When making phone calls, you may use any of the following questions (or one of your own) as a conversation starter:

• Do you have any specific questions about ministry opportunities at our church?

- Have you and your family decided about your response to the stewardship program?
- Have you received a pledge card?

Here are some possible responses for callers:

If they say, "Yes, we are planning to make a pledge."

Affirm their decision and thank them for their participation. Encourage them to return their card on or before the next weekend.

If they say, "No, we are not going to make a pledge at this time."

This is your opportunity to be caring and supportive. Thank them and be gracious. Do not try to convince them to make a pledge; simply ask them to pray for the ministries and future of the church.

If they say, "We will give, but we will not specify an amount."

In some churches, this is a part of the giving culture. If you feel comfortable in doing so, tell them a statement of intent (aka a pledge card) enables your leadership to be better stewards of the church's resources.

If they say, "We haven't made a decision yet."

Offer to answer any questions they may have or find someone who has the information they need. Sometimes you can be of help simply by listening.

It is likely you will connect with voice mail or answering machines. If so, we suggest you use the following guidelines:

First time: "This is Jane Doe. I'm calling from ABC Church. I'll call back again."

Second time: "This is Jane Doe from the stewardship committee at ABC Church. Would you please call me at 555-1212?"

Third time: "This is Jane Doe from the stewardship committee at ABC Church. I'm calling because we are hoping you are planning to support the ministries of our church with a pledge this year. If you could please call and let me know your plans, I would appreciate it. We are hoping to celebrate the results of this year's campaign on _____ and would love for you to be a part of it. I hope you will prayerfully consider joining us in this effort. Please feel free to call me at 555-1212 if you have any questions."

If you have reached the answering machine on all three tries, do not call back.

3. The Pledge Card

Some important elements to consider when designing your pledge card:

1. Keep it simple and easy to complete.

2. We recommend you do not take pledges for time and talent at the same time as monetary pledges. For some it becomes a pledging of time, talent, *or* treasure. As you know, pledging of treasure can be the most difficult.

3. If you are planning to distribute and collect pledge cards as an act of worship, it may be helpful to publish a picture of the pledge card you will be using in your newsletter or bulletin. That way

people will know what to expect and will be better prepared to complete their pledge cards in worship.

4. Do not use green or neon-colored stock for your pledge cards. Green tends to make people think of money and the neon stock is difficult on the eyes. Cream or off-white tends to work best.

5. Pledge cards can be easily copied in-house—usually three per 8½ x 11 page. They should fit into a #9 envelope for return to the church.

Sample Pledge Card:

St. Swithin's Church

Every generous act of giving, with every perfect gift, is from above,
coming down from the Father of lights.

—James 1:17

I/We wish to pledge $_____ to St. Swithin's for the 20[XX] calendar year.

I/We do not usually make a financial pledge, but for budgeting purposes you can count on me/us to contribute $_____ to St. Swithin's for the 20[XX] calendar year.

_____ This represents an increase in giving.

(Please print)

Name(s)

_____

Address

_____

City   State   Zip

_____   _____   _____

E-mail(s)

_____

Phone

_____

_____ Please send information on conributing stocks, mutual funds, or opportunities to make a planned gift to the church.

_____ Please send information about direct deposit or electronic funds transfer for my/our pledge.

Your generosity changes lives through the ministries of our church. Your pledge may be revised if necessary.

Notes

Introduction

1. Explorersweb, www.mounteverest.net/expguide/dream.htm.
2. Bob Doucette, " 'Everest Beyond the Limit' Returns; Some Thoughts on the First Three Episodes," *Out There* (blog), December 28, 2009, http://blog.newsok.com/outthere/2009/12/.
3. Explorersweb, www.mounteverest.net/expguide/dream.htm.

1. Clear and Compelling Vision

1. Jon Krakauer, *Into Thin Air* (New York: Random House, 1997), 136.
2. Giving USA Foundation, 2009 Survey.
3. Henri J. M. Nouwen, *A Spirituality of Fundraising*, ed. John S. Mogabgab (Nashville: Upper Room Books, 2010), 16–17.
4. National Geographic News, October 4, 2002, http://news.national geographic.com/news/2002/10/1004_021004_kroppclimber.html.
5. Percept, www.perceptgroup.com.

2. Leadership Development

1. Jon Krakauer, *Into Thin Air* (New York: Random House, 1997), 29–30.

2. Tom Peters, *Re-imagine: Business Excellence in a Disruptive Age* (New York: DK Publishing, 2006), 342.

3. Inspiration

1. Henri J. M. Nouwen, *A Spirituality of Fundraising*, ed. John S. Mogabgab (Nashville: Upper Room Books, 2010), 17–18.
2. Ibid., 33.
3. United States Conference of Catholic Bishops, *Stewardship: A Disciple's Response*, www.nccbuscc.org/stewardship/disciplesresponse.pdf.
4. Ibid.

4. Motivation

1. Jon Krakauer, *Into Thin Air* (New York: Random House, 1997), 136.
2. Henri J. M. Nouwen, *A Spirituality of Fundraising* (Nashville: Upper Room Books, 2010), 16–17.
3. George Barna, "Tithing Down 62% in the Past Year," May 19, 2003, www.barna.org/barna-update/article/5-barna-update/121-tithing-down-62-in-the-past-year.

5. Boldly Ask

1. www.pbs.org/wgbh/nova/everest/climb/waytosummitsou.html. Accessed April 26, 2011.
2. Pew Forum on Religion & Public Life, *Religion Among the Millennials* (Washington, DC: February 2010).
3. Barna Group, "A New Generation Expresses Its Skepticism and Frustration with Christianity," September 24, 2007, www.barna.org/barna-update/article/16-teensnext-gen/94-a-new-generation-expresses-its-skepticism-and-frustration-with-christianity.